13 Things STRONG KIDS DO

THINK BIG, Feel GOOD, ACT BRAVE

13 Things STRONG KIDS DO

THINK BIG, Feel GOOD, ACT BRAVE

AMY MORIN

ILLUSTRATED BY JENNIFER NAALCHIGAR

HARPER

An Imprint of HarperCollinsPublishers

First Edition

To all the kids
who want to become a little stronger today
than they were yesterday

Contents

13 Things STRONG KIDS DO

THINK BIG, Feel GOOD, ACT BRAVE

Introduction

A while back, I wrote a book called *13 Things Mentally Strong People Don't Do*. It was a book for adults about how to get rid of bad habits. But readers kept saying the same thing about it: "I wish I had learned these things back when I was a kid."

So I wrote *this* book specifically for kids! We're going to talk about how to start good habits now so you don't build bad habits later. Your future self will thank you for reading it today!

But before we talk about those good habits, let's talk a little about what it means to be strong in the first place.

There are lots of different kinds of strength. You might be the kind of strong kid who has big muscles and can lift heavy things. Or maybe you're a strong

1

student who does really well in every class.

Those kinds of strengths can be helpful in life. But they're not what we are going to talk about here.

Instead, we're going to talk about mental strength. If you aren't sure what that means, don't worry! You're not alone. Many adults aren't quite sure, either.

Mental strength is what it takes to become your best self. Building mental muscle requires you to pay attention to three things: the way you think, feel, and act.

Thinking big, feeling good, and acting brave will all help you develop bigger mental muscles. And when you have bigger mental muscles, it's easier to think big, feel good, and act brave! It's a two-way street.

THE LINK BETWEEN THOUGHTS, FEELINGS, AND ACTIONS

Look at it this way. Your thoughts, feelings, and actions are all connected, and they create a cycle that can either be positive or negative.

Here's an example:

SITUATION: It's raining outside.
KID #1:
- **Thinks:** "This is terrible. I can't go outside and have fun!"
- **Feels:** sad, bored, angry

- **Acts:** He sits inside all day, staring out the window and sulking.

KID #2:

- **Thinks:** "I guess I can't play outside. I'll see if I can have a friend come over instead."
- **Feels:** happy, hopeful, excited
- **Acts:** She invites a friend over, and they have fun together.

Which kid feels better? Clearly, kid number two! That kid found a way to make the best of the situation.

In real life, of course, we get caught in situations that are more complex than rainy days.

But if you develop healthy habits to make the best of those situations, you will build your mental muscles until you can handle almost any challenge life throws your way.

So that's what this book is about. Each chapter will teach you how to think big, feel good, and act brave—so you can become the strongest and best version of yourself!

BEING STRONG VS. ACTING TOUGH

Before we learn how to become stronger, let's get one thing clear: being strong is not the same as acting tough.

Many people—including adults—get confused about what it means to be a strong kid.

A parent who doesn't understand what it means to be strong might tell their kids, "Stop crying! Crying is for babies!" But crying isn't a sign of weakness. And it's not just for babies, either. Sometimes tears can be a sign of strength!

Strong people show their feelings. People who are just acting tough pretend they don't even have feelings. They're more likely to say, "I don't care. That doesn't bother me," even when they feel sad about something.

Sometimes people think being strong means acting like a bully. But that's definitely not true! The reason most bullies try to control other people is because they can't control their *own* thoughts, feelings, and actions. Strong people focus on controlling themselves instead of others.

Here are some more key differences between being strong and acting tough:

KIDS WHO ARE WORKING ON BEING STRONG:

They want to become better. They say things like, "I could really work on my self-confidence!"

KIDS WHO ARE TRYING TO LOOK TOUGH:

They deny that they have anything to work on. They say things like, "I'm perfect just the way I am."

KIDS WHO ARE WORKING ON BEING STRONG:

They acknowledge and express their feelings.

KIDS WHO ARE TRYING TO LOOK TOUGH:

They pretend they don't have feelings (except maybe for anger).

KIDS WHO ARE WORKING ON BEING STRONG:

They focus on becoming better on the inside. They aren't worried about how they look to other people.

KIDS WHO ARE TRYING TO LOOK TOUGH:

They work hard to look like they are doing well on the outside. They worry a lot about what other people think.

KIDS WHO ARE WORKING ON BEING STRONG:

They are interested in liking themselves. They care about their own character.

KIDS WHO ARE TRYING TO LOOK TOUGH:

They are mostly interested in making sure other people like them. They care more about their reputation.

KIDS WHO ARE WORKING ON BEING STRONG:

They believe that mistakes and failures can make them better.

KIDS WHO ARE TRYING TO LOOK TOUGH:

They believe that only losers fail. They hide their mistakes.

As you have probably figured out by now, mental strength isn't about thinking everything is great, pretending to feel happy all the time, or acting like you don't have any problems.

It's about learning how to think, feel, and act in a way that helps you become your best self.

It's also about liking who you are now and trying to become even better!

MENTAL STRENGTH TRAINING

Each chapter of this book talks about one thing strong kids do. When you are reading, you might think, "Oh no, I don't do this!" Don't worry. None of us do these things all the time (not even adults).

That doesn't mean you're not strong. No one is perfect! We all have room for improvement.

And that's what this book is for. Each chapter will show you exercises that can help you grow a little stronger. With practice, you'll find it's easier to start doing the things strong kids do.

That's because mental strength is a lot like physical strength. If you want to have bigger physical muscles, you need to lift weights.

If you want bigger mental muscles, you need to exercise, too. But don't worry, this book won't ask you to do any jumping jacks or run any sprints. We're talking about mental exercises here!

Some of the exercises will teach you ways to *solve a problem*. Other exercises will show you ways to *solve how you feel about a problem*. This is because some problems can be solved, and others can't.

Here's an example of the difference:

If you have fallen behind on your homework, you might feel bad. The best way to respond to a problem like this is to figure out how to get caught up on your work. Then you'll feel better. It's a problem you can solve.

But if you feel bad because your mom is sick, you

can't fix that. You might be able to bring her chicken soup to help her feel better, but you can't make her illness disappear. So you might find it helpful to do an exercise that helps you worry a little less or feel a little less sad. This could help you solve how you feel about the problem.

So when you are feeling bad about something, ask yourself, "Do I need to solve the problem? Or do I need to solve how I feel about the problem?" Then choose the exercises that are most likely to help you.

Let's do a little warm-up now before we get started with Chapter 1. Here are three exercises that will prepare you for the rest of this book and increase your chances of success!

Are you ready to get started?

THINK BIG

PLAY TO WIN

Imagine an Olympic track star stepping up to the starting line. This person is known for winning almost every race he runs because he's so fast! Now imagine a great soccer player stepping onto the field for a big game. This player is known for being one of the greatest because she has scored so many goals in her career! What do you think is running through those superstars' heads before they get ready to compete? Are they thinking, "I seriously hope I don't lose today"? Or do you imagine they're thinking, "I've got this. I've trained hard, and I'm ready to do my best"?

If you guessed the second one, you're probably right. Most great athletes get to where they are because they "think big." And in their case, that means they're playing to win!

Scientists have found that the way we think affects our performance. When our goal is just to "not embarrass ourselves," we don't do as well as when our goal is "to break a record."

This strategy can help you perform better in any part of your life. Whether you're shooting a foul shot, giving a speech, or starting a conversation with the new kid in your school, tell yourself you're going to do well. You will increase your chances of success!

Do that right now with this book, too. Instead of thinking, "Oh no, all of this sounds too tough. I can't do it," tell yourself something like, "This sounds challenging. But I'm ready!" Thinking big like that will help you grow stronger, starting now.

Feel GOOD

NAME FIVE TRUSTED PEOPLE YOU CAN TALK TO

Some of the exercises in this book may stir up some uncomfortable feelings. They might cause you to think about difficult things or take actions that seem kind of tough.

There may be times that you feel a little stuck. Or you might not know what to do with the thoughts and feelings you're having. That's when it's important to have adults you can talk to. An adult can help you find healthy ways to deal with these challenges.

Remember, feeling anxious or depressed isn't a sign of weakness. You might be physically strong and still get a physical health problem (like a bad cold), right? In the same way, mental muscles will help you stay strong, but they don't guarantee you won't ever have a mental health problem. If you struggle with a mental health issue, you may need an adult or a doctor to help you feel better.

Before you start this book, create a list of five trusted adults you can talk to if you need a little help along the way. Your list might include parents, teachers, coaches, doctors, guidance counselors, or maybe even your friends' parents. Just think of people who you know would help you if you asked.

1. _____

2. _____

3. _____

4. _____

5. _____

ACT BRAVE

PERFORM EXPERIMENTS

Finally, this book is going to ask you to try a lot of new things. You might find yourself thinking they won't work for you, or you might try something once and decide there's no use in attempting it again.

This book will work best if you act like a scientist testing experiments. Try every exercise in each chapter. Try each one at least a few times. Pay attention to whether the exercises help you get stronger. If they do, then keep on going with them!

If you find an exercise or two that just don't seem right for you, that's okay, as long as you tried your best. You might find that certain exercises just aren't a good fit. You can decide to focus more on the exercises that work better for you.

But remember, your job is to conduct the experiments. You won't know if the exercises work until you try them.

HOW THIS BOOK WORKS

In each chapter, you'll discover a thing that strong kids do. You'll meet a kid who struggled with that thing. And you'll follow their journey as they learn to grow stronger. Here's what else you can expect in each chapter:

 Check Yourself—A short, easy quiz that will help you learn more about yourself.

 Closer Look—A deeper look at how to learn the things strong kids do.

 PROOF POSITIVE—Evidence that shows why a certain good habit can help you in life.

Exercises—There are three exercises in each chapter that will help you:

> **THINK BIG**—You'll learn how to deal with the tricks your brain tries to play on you.

> **Feel GOOD**—You'll discover how to deal with uncomfortable emotions and how to feel your best.

> **ACT BRAVE**—You'll practice doing things that help you become your best.

Traps to Avoid—Common mistakes and misunder-standings.

 QUICK TIPS—Short reminders for how you can keep growing stronger.

There will be times when some of these things seem easy. And there will be other times when they feel really tough. Don't worry! We are all a work in progress.

With practice, you'll learn how to think, feel, and act stronger than ever!

1

They Stop Feeling Sorry for Themselves

Hailey loved to sing and entertain people. When she was a little girl, she would sing in the shower. She would even sing in front of the mirror and pretend her hairbrush was the microphone. She threw concerts for her parents and her younger sisters. And when she got older, she sang in church. Hailey just loved performing!

That's why she was so excited about the school chorus concert coming up. Five kids were going to get picked to sing a few lines all by themselves in the show. Hailey wanted her chance to sing in the spotlight in front of the whole school!

She had never sung in front of a large crowd before. She imagined all the people who would likely come to hear her sing—her family, her grandparents, and maybe even her neighbors.

She picked out the dress she would wear. She decided how she would do her hair on the big night, too. She needed to look good, after all. This was going to be her big moment!

All the kids who wanted a solo part had to try out for it. Fifteen kids were trying out, and there were just five parts.

When tryouts came around, Hailey felt pretty nervous. Then she listened to her first classmate sing. Hailey thought, "He sounds off-key."

Another girl stepped up. Hailey's friend leaned over and whispered, "She sounds like she's screeching!" Hailey giggled—even though she tried not to.

Finally it was Hailey's turn to sing. She walked to the front of the room and looked her chorus teacher right in the eyes, just as she had practiced. She cleared her throat and sang her heart out!

When she was done, her teacher nodded and smiled. He motioned for Hailey to have a seat. Hailey felt good about her performance. She felt sure her teacher's smile meant she had gotten one of the solo parts.

The next morning Hailey went straight to her chorus teacher's office. He had promised to post the list of soloists. She saw the paper taped to the outside of his door. Hailey scanned the list but couldn't find her name.

Was there some mistake? She knew she'd done a good job. She read the list again, just to be certain. As she did, one of the seventh graders came along and said to her, "Hey, look! I got a part! Did you?"

Hailey shook her head as her eyes filled up with tears.

The rest of the day felt like a blur. She was sad she wasn't picked. She was also angry at her teacher. Why did he smile at her if he wasn't going to give her a part?

When she got off the bus after the long day of school, she ran through her front door. As soon as she stepped inside, she yelled, "Mom, I'm never singing again! No one likes my voice! My teacher made me try out for a part he knew I wasn't going to get! This whole thing was a bad idea!"

Her mother tried to find out what happened. But before she could ask many questions, Hailey ran to her bedroom and shut the door. She didn't ever want to come out.

Check Yourself

Just like Hailey, everyone feels sorry for themselves sometimes. When you catch yourself doing this, however, it's important to stop—otherwise, your feelings can get bigger and last longer. That's when they can become a big problem. Take a look at the sentences below. How many of these things sound like you?

- [ ] I only ever have bad luck.
- [ ] I complain a lot about things being unfair.
- [ ] I think my problems are bigger than everyone else's.
- [ ] I feel like no one understands how hard my life really is.
- [ ] I think more about things that go wrong than things that go right.
- [ ] Sometimes I think the universe is against me.
- [ ] I often think nothing good will ever happen to me.

Do you say many of these things to yourself? If you do, you might be feeling sorry for yourself a little too much. It's what the experts call self-pity. Self-pity isn't the same as being sad. We'll talk more about that in just a little bit. In this chapter, we'll talk about how to recognize self-pity and try some exercises that will help you stop feeling sorry for yourself.

But first, let's get back to Hailey and the solo part. . . .

 ## Closer Look

Hailey felt devastated when she didn't get a solo. She locked herself in her room. She convinced herself that everyone hated her voice. She was going to give up singing forever and hide from the world!

That's when she crossed over from healthy sadness to unhealthy self-pity. Hailey began to exaggerate how bad her life was.

It's easy for anyone to do what Hailey did. It happens when we confuse sadness with self-pity, even though they are two very different things.

Being sad can be good for you. It can help you remember something you lost, for instance. When you are sad about a friend who moved away, you might remember to reach out to them.

If you feel sad about your pet who died, you might remember how much fun you had while they were alive. You might enjoy looking at old pictures of you two. Letting yourself feel sad about things like these helps you heal.

But self-pity is different. When you have self-pity, you overestimate how big your problems are and underestimate your ability to handle them. You might even start to feel hopeless.

Here are some examples that show the difference between sad thoughts and self-pity thoughts:

SITUATION: Your best friend moves away.

- **Sad Thought:** "I'm going to miss seeing my friend at school every day."

- **Self-pity Thought:** "I'll never make another friend again! I'll be alone every day."

SITUATION: You didn't make the basketball team.
- **Sad Thought:** "I'm so bummed that I won't be able to play on the team this season."
- **Self-pity Thought:** "I never get picked for anything! I'm never going to try out again."

SITUATION: It's raining, and your friend's outdoor party got canceled.
- **Sad Thought:** "I'm sad that I can't see my friends today. That party was going to be so much fun."
- **Self-pity Thought:** "Nothing ever goes right! Even when we have something fun planned, it always gets ruined!"

REFLECTION:

What's an example of a sad thought you've had?

_____

_____

What's an example of a self-pity thought you've had?

_____

_____

PROOF POSITIVE

When Hailey felt sorry for herself, she stopped talking to everyone. She locked herself in her room and climbed into bed.

She kept thinking about how horrible her life was and how unfair the chorus teacher was. Doing nothing gave her more time to focus on her negative thoughts. It made her feel even worse. And the worse she felt, the less likely she was to do anything that might get her out of her rut.

In a strange way, she thought her self-pity was going to protect her from feeling sad and embarrassed. It's as if she was saying, "Oh yeah, if my teacher doesn't want me to have a solo part, I'll punish everyone by never singing again!"

Self-pity can make us think some pretty bizarre things.

Hailey got caught in this downward spiral because she believed the negative thoughts . . . and they just weren't true. She wasn't the world's worst singer. Not even close.

Believing your negative thoughts can lead to more self-pity, which leads to more negative thoughts. And the longer this goes on, the less likely you are to fix anything. It's a tough cycle to break.

21

Here are some more reasons why self-pity just doesn't work:

- It makes you feel worse.
- It doesn't fix the problem.
- It wastes time.

REFLECTION:

What's a time when you felt sorry for yourself?

_____

_____

How did self-pity make your situation worse?

_____

_____

HOW DID HAILEY GROW STRONGER?

The more time Hailey spent in her room, the worse she felt. She threw away notebooks of her favorite song lyrics. She ripped down the posters of her favorite singers. She even deleted some music from her computer! She didn't want to be near anything that reminded her of singing or tryouts or the concert.

Hailey found her favorite picture in her dresser. It

was of her as a little girl singing in her pajamas. Just as she was about to rip it up, her mother knocked on the door. She came in to remind Hailey to do her chores.

Hailey responded by saying, "Mom, how can you expect me to do those things today? All my dreams just got ruined! I'm never going to be a singer! Don't you understand?"

Calmly, her mother replied, "I'm sorry that you didn't get a solo part in the concert. I know it was really important to you. I would feel sad and hurt too. I also know that you are a great singer. You can still make music a big part of your life. You just didn't get this one part!"

This was not what Hailey wanted to hear. She wanted her mother to say that her teacher was stupid for not seeing her talent. Better yet, she wanted her mother to say she was going to march down to the school to talk to him! Maybe her mom could convince him that Hailey deserved a solo part.

She wanted her mother to give up music, too. That's right, Hailey thought. She never wanted her mother to turn on the radio or make a new playlist again.

Hailey's mother didn't do any of those things, however. Instead, she told Hailey she needed to vacuum the living room.

Of course, Hailey didn't feel like doing chores. But she also didn't want to get grounded. So she went downstairs and got the vacuum cleaner out.

But something happened once she started cleaning. Almost automatically, Hailey started singing.

She stopped as soon as she noticed she was doing it. After all, she never wanted to sing again. But a few minutes later, she was singing another song as she swept the bathroom floor. She always sang when she cleaned. It was a habit.

To her surprise, she felt a little bit better when she sang. So, she figured she could just sing really quietly so her mother wouldn't hear her. *(She wanted her mother to think she'd quit music forever, right?)*

The next day her chorus teacher told the class that everyone who tried out for solo parts did a good job. It had been a tough decision to make, he explained. Then he said, "If you didn't get a solo part this time, don't worry. There will be plenty more chances in the future."

Hearing him say that changed how Hailey felt. Maybe it wasn't right to think her teacher was mean and unfair. Deep down, she still thought he was a good teacher. And when he said it had been a tough

decision, she believed him.

"Maybe I didn't have the right range for the singing parts on these songs," she thought. That idea was the first step to stopping her self-pity in its tracks.

Hailey was still sad that she wouldn't get to step onto the big stage this time. But she decided to keep practicing anyway. Maybe her big chance was right around the corner.

Exercises

THINK BIG

TURN "BLUE THOUGHTS" INTO TRUE THOUGHTS

Hailey's brain played tricks on her. It tried to tell her that she should never sing again just because she didn't get one solo part! Those negative thoughts she was having are "BLUE thoughts."

You can probably relate to this. When you are in a bad mood, your brain may try to tell you that things are worse than they really are. Luckily, not everything you think is true!

Here's what BLUE stands for:

- Blaming everyone
- Looking for bad news
- Unhappy guessing
- Exaggerating

When you notice yourself experiencing BLUE thoughts, replace them with true thoughts.

Blaming everyone

Problems aren't all someone else's fault. They aren't all your fault, either. So make sure you don't *Blame everyone* else. But don't blame yourself more than necessary, either. Take responsibility for your share.

- **BLUE thought:** "My teacher never tells me what to study."
- **True thought:** "I can ask the teacher questions if I don't understand."

Looking for bad news

Think about your day at school right now. Do you remember the worst things that happened? Or do you remember the good stuff, too?

Here is an example: Let's say you met ten kids today. Eight were nice to you. Two of them were mean. Your parents ask how your day was.

- **BLUE thought:** "The kids were all so mean!"
- **True thought:** "Most of the kids were nice."

Do you talk about the eight nice kids? Or do you talk about the two mean kids?

If you're *Looking for bad news*, then you will talk mostly about the two mean kids. And that will keep you stuck in a bad mood!

So try to look for the good. Remind yourself that some bad things are going to happen sometimes. But there will be good things, too!

Unhappy guessing

No one knows for sure what's going to happen in the future. But sometimes we make guesses that make us feel bad. Maybe you think that you're going to fail a test. Or maybe you assume no one is going to talk to you at your new school. Thoughts like these are *Unhappy guessing*. Here's an example:

- **BLUE thought:** "I'm going to mess up tomorrow."
- **True thought:** "I'll do my best tomorrow."

Don't believe all your catastrophic predictions. Instead, think about the steps you could take to stop bad things from happening. Maybe you can study for a test so you don't fail. Or you can practice being a good friend to other people so that you aren't all alone.

Exaggerating

Some thoughts are too negative to be true. You might think, "No one ever likes me!" or "I'm never going to pass math class!" Thoughts like these are self-pity.

When you think like this, you are experiencing *Exaggerated negative thoughts.*

If you catch yourself thinking, "Everything bad always happens to me!" then remember the good things that have happened. If you think, "Nothing ever goes right!" then make a list of things that do go right.

- BLUE thought: "No one ever likes me."
- True thought: "Some people like me."

When your thoughts get gloomy, ask yourself, "Is this a BLUE thought or a true thought?" Look for any evidence that your thought might be BLUE. And then look for any evidence that it might be true.

For example, if you think you'll never pass math, what's the evidence this is true? Maybe you failed one test. Now what's the evidence that it's not true? Maybe you got a good grade on your homework last week.

After you look at the evidence, then ask yourself how you can let a true thought replace the BLUE thought. You might decide that you struggle a little with math, but you can still choose to study hard and do your best. Reminding yourself of these true thoughts can help you feel better!

REFLECTION:

What's an example of a BLUE thought you've had recently?

_____

_____

Now replace that BLUE thought with a true thought!

_____

_____

Feel GOOD

ARE YOUR FEELINGS A FRIEND OR AN ENEMY?

At first, Hailey's sadness was her friend. She was experiencing normal feelings after missing out on her big solo.

But when she crossed into self-pity, her feelings became her enemy. She was ripping up her stuff, saying she was never going to sing again, and daydreaming about her mother yelling at her teacher. None of those things were helpful.

Learning to recognize when your feelings are helpful and when they become hurtful is important.

Every feeling can be helpful to you sometimes. But

that same feeling can be hurtful to you other times. Feelings aren't always either good or bad.

If your feeling is "a friend," keep feeling it. If it is "an enemy," change how you feel (we'll talk more about that in the "Act Brave" section).

Here's how any feeling can be a friend or an enemy:

Happiness

FRIEND—Happiness can be your friend when it helps you be friendly, think positive thoughts, and have fun.

ENEMY—Happiness might be an enemy if it causes you to forget about the things that could go wrong and you take a giant risk without considering the consequences.

Sadness

FRIEND—Sadness might be your friend when it helps you appreciate what you still have. If you're sad after a friend moves away, you might start to appreciate your other friends even more.

ENEMY—Sadness might be an enemy if it causes you to stay in your room by yourself all the time.

Anger

FRIEND—Anger can be your friend when it gives you the courage to stand up for a kid who is getting bullied.

ENEMY—Anger might be your enemy if it causes you to say mean things that hurt someone's feelings.

Anxiety

FRIEND—Anxiety can be your friend when it keeps you safe from harm. If your friend dares you to jump off a bridge, your anxiety might remind you that's a bad idea because you could get hurt.

ENEMY—Anxiety might be your enemy if it keeps you from being in the science fair because you think your project might not be good enough.

When sadness crosses over into self-pity, it becomes an enemy. It can keep you stuck in a dark place. It's important to recognize when you're feeling sorry for yourself, so that you can get unstuck.

REFLECTION:

Think about what you're feeling right now. Is this emo-tion your friend or your enemy?

_____

_____

ACT BRAVE

PICK A MOOD BOOSTER

If Hailey had stayed in her room all night, she would have stayed stuck in a bad mood. She only started feeling better when she got up and started cleaning. And while cleaning isn't exactly fun, it was better than ripping up her pictures and throwing away her notebooks. When she was cleaning, she started singing. And when she started singing, she felt happier.

When you are feeling sorry for yourself, you might feel tempted to do things that keep you stuck in a bad mood. You might sulk, sit around by yourself, or complain about how unfair your life is.

But the best way to help yourself feel better is to do things that make you happy. Dance around the house! Jump on your trampoline! Do whatever you think is fun. It will boost your mood even when you don't feel like doing those things.

We call those things that make you feel happier mood boosters. These are the things you usually enjoy doing when you feel happy. Here is a sample list of one kid's mood boosters:

1. Playing with my dog
2. Singing
3. Shooting hoops
4. Playing a game with my sibling
5. Going for a walk outside
6. Baking cookies
7. Drawing
8. Talking to my friends
9. Reading funny books
10. Watching funny videos online

Now think about all the things *you* like to do when you're happy. What do you do for fun when you come home from school in a good mood? What do you like to do outside when you're happy? What are some things you can do in your room when you're happy? These are going to be your own personal mood boosters.

Create your list of mood boosters:

1. _____
2. _____
3. _____
4. _____
5. _____
6. _____
7. _____
8. _____
9. _____
10. _____

Keep this list close by! Hang it in your room or put it on your nightstand. The next time you're feeling down, do one of the activities on your list. It might help you feel better fast!

Traps to Avoid

There may be times when you think, "I'm not exaggerating the bad things. They really are this bad!"

And there may be days when you are absolutely right. During those times, feeling sad might be helpful. But remember that no matter how bad things are, feeling sorry for yourself will only make things worse.

You also could have a friend who seems to feel sorry for themselves a lot. When they're having a hard time, you might ask how you can help them feel better. But when they're in the middle of feeling sorry for themselves, they may not really want your help. They might want to just stay stuck. That's okay. All you can do is offer.

There will likely be times that you just can't seem to get unstuck yourself, no matter how hard you try. If you are really struggling to stop feeling sorry for yourself, talk to an adult you trust.

Tell a parent or a teacher about how you're feeling. They may be able to help you, or find someone who can.

QUICK TIPS

Strong kids stop feeling sorry for themselves. Clearly, that's hard to do sometimes. But now that you know how to recognize self-pity and you know the exercises that can help you get unstuck, you can choose to stop feeling sorry for yourself, too. Here's a reminder of those exercises that can help you think big, feel good, and act brave.

THINK BIG: Notice when your thoughts are too negative to be true. Replace your BLUE thoughts with true thoughts.

Feel GOOD : Ask yourself if your feelings are a friend or an enemy.

ACT BRAVE : Make a list of ten mood boosters. When you're feeling stuck in a bad mood, pick a mood booster to help you feel better.

2

They Empower Themselves

Jayden woke up on his last day of summer vacation wishing he could make his break last just a little longer. Tomorrow was his first day of junior high, and he was dreading it.

Not too long ago, he actually liked school. He got good grades and he had lots of friends.

But things changed last year when his friends started teasing him all the time. For some reason, they liked making him look stupid. They'd ask questions like, "Who won the football game last night?" or, "Which basketball player was the highest scorer last year?"

Jayden never knew the answers. He didn't even like professional sports.

At first he would simply say, "I don't know." But when he admitted that he didn't know, his friends cracked up.

So he tried a new plan. He answered their questions by saying, "I don't want to talk about that right now." But his friends still made fun of him.

Finally he tried saying, "You're only asking that because you don't know the answer either!" That just made them laugh even harder.

Jayden felt so stupid that he made a plan to stop the mocking. He studied sports so he could answer any questions that came his way. He watched NFL games, read articles about NBA players, and collected baseball cards. He still didn't like sports, but he was sick of not fitting in with the other guys.

When he tried to show off his new knowledge, it didn't go well. At the lunch table, he said, "I think the Cowboys are going all the way this year!"

One of his friends chuckled and said, "Yeah? Why don't you tell us how many times they won the Super Bowl already?"

When he couldn't answer, another friend said, "Jayden learns one random football fact, and now he thinks he's an expert!"

It had been an awful experience and Jayden didn't

want to go through anything like that ever again. But now he was headed to junior high! What if things were about to get even worse?

He pictured his friends laughing at him in the hallways. He imagined them telling everyone on the bus that he didn't know the difference between the Yankees and the Red Sox. And he pictured them calling him names when he couldn't recall the latest football stats.

As he thought more of the awful things that awaited him at school this year, Jayden pulled the blankets up over his head. All he wanted to do on his last day of summer vacation was to figure out how to get out of going back to school.

Check Yourself

You are in control of how you think, feel, and behave. But there might be times when you give someone else power over your thoughts, feelings, and behaviors. Check out these sentences. How many of them sound like you?

- ☐ I get so angry at other people that I say and do mean things.
- ☐ How I feel about myself depends on how other people feel about me.
- ☐ I believe people who criticize me.

☐ I act how I think other kids want me to act.

☐ Sometimes I do things I wouldn't normally do because I'm trying to fit in.

☐ My mood depends on the mood of people around me.

☐ If another kid makes fun of me for something, I try to change it.

How true do those things sound about you? The more they sound like you, the more likely you are to give away your personal power. We all do this sometimes, but doing it too much can be a real problem. In this chapter, we'll talk about how to know when you're giving people power over you. Then we will find out how you can *keep* your power, or empower yourself. When you learn to do this, you will get stronger and feel better!

But first, let's go back to Jayden and the trouble with his friends. . . .

Closer Look

Jayden knew he couldn't hide forever, but he didn't know what else to do. He had given his friends power over the way he felt about himself and about school. He even let them control how he behaved.

Here's how Jayden gave his friends power over him:

JAYDEN'S THOUGHTS

When Jayden's friends teased him, he started thinking things like, "I'm so stupid! I must be a nerd since I don't like sports." He also pictured the guys teasing him even worse.

JAYDEN'S FEELINGS

Jayden felt sad and embarrassed. He began dreading school! He was always scared that his friends would start in again at any moment.

JAYDEN'S ACTIONS

He started watching and studying sports even though he didn't really like them. Instead of having fun on his last day of summer vacation, he stayed in bed all day.

Jayden allowed his friends to affect his school life and his home life. He felt stuck because he let them take away his power. He needed to learn to empower himself!

But before we talk about how to empower yourself, it's important to understand the difference between giving away your power and empowering yourself. Here are some examples:

SITUATION: Someone says the food you bring for lunch is weird.

- **Giving away your power:** "I'm never packing a lunch like this again!"

- **Empowering yourself:** "I like this food. I'm going to keep bringing it for lunch!"

SITUATION: You see a popular kid wearing a certain type of jacket that you don't really like.

- **Giving away your power:** "That must be the jacket to wear right now. I'm going to ask my parents to buy me one just like it."

- **Empowering yourself:** "That jacket is right for her. But I like my own style!"

SITUATION: Your friend says vaping is cool and you should try it.

- **Giving away your power:** "I know I shouldn't do this. But I don't want to look lame. I think I'm going to try it."

- **Empowering yourself:** "I know this is very bad for me, and I could get addicted. There's no way I'm trying it!"

Giving away your power might not seem like a big deal sometimes. But there are many reasons why it's important to empower yourself! We'll talk about those reasons next.

REFLECTION:

Think of a time when you let someone have power over you. What could you have done to empower yourself?

_____

_____

PROOF POSITIVE

Why did Jayden feel so miserable? It was because the kids he called "friends" were treating him horribly. He spent a lot of time trying to change himself so they would stop teasing him.

But the more he tried to learn about sports, the worse he felt.

He was learning about sports because he was trying to impress his friends. That whole time he could have been doing something he actually liked. Then he would have been feeling much happier!

When you keep your power, you become the driver in your life instead of the passenger. Here's why:

- You decide how you feel about yourself.
- You decide what kind of day you're going to have.
- You form your own opinions.
- You determine your mood.
- You set the rules for how other people treat you.

When you empower yourself, you don't depend on other people to feel good. You can decide to feel good even when someone else is in a bad mood. And you can decide who you want to be friends with, too.

Empowering yourself helps you be the strongest version of you. You'll feel more comfortable being yourself when you have power.

REFLECTION:

Think about how your life could be different in the future if you keep your power.

How might you think differently?

_____

_____

How might you feel differently?

_____

_____

What might you do differently?

_____

_____

HOW DID JAYDEN GROW STRONGER?

Jayden walked into junior high filled with anxiety. He kept thinking, "Just get through the day without getting picked on!"

He found his homeroom. He walked in and looked around nervously. He didn't know anyone. But when Jayden found his desk, the kid next to him said, "What's up? I'm Terrance. I guess I'm sitting next to you."

Jayden noticed the kid was wearing a T-shirt with his favorite band on it. "You like them?" he asked. He didn't know anyone else who did.

"Yeah, I love them!" Terrance said. "I went to their show this summer. It was epic!"

The two boys spent the next ten minutes talking about their favorite music.

When the bell rang, Terrance said, "Hey, come sit with us at lunch!"

Jayden's first reaction was to say, "Nah, I'm going to sit with my friends." But before the words came out of his mouth, he remembered that his "friends" made lunch miserable most of the time. So he said, "Sure! Why not? See you there."

In that moment, Jayden realized maybe his old friends were not as important as he thought. If they really liked him, they wouldn't make fun of him. Today he would not give them any power.

That didn't mean his old friends were all bad. He could still hang out with them sometimes if he wanted to. But now he knew he could make new friends, too! It was awesome when he found new people who were into the same things he was. And he felt good about himself when he made his own choices.

Jayden felt relieved. For the first time, he was excited about junior high. He thought, "Maybe this year will be great after all!"

Exercises

THINK BIG

CREATE YOUR CATCHPHRASE

Jayden had spent a lot of time thinking about the hurtful things his friends had said to him. And even when he was hanging out with them, he was always worried that they were going to ask him about sports again. He had to change his thinking to feel better.

It's tough to drown out negative thoughts—especially when other people say mean things. When someone else calls you names or insults you, you might find their words swirling around in your head. And each time you think of them, you probably feel bad all over again. That way of thinking gives people power over you. You don't want those negative people taking up space in your brain!

Creating a catchphrase can help you drown out those negative thoughts and empower you to feel better. Your catchphrase is a short saying you can repeat to yourself whenever you need a little pep talk.

The best catchphrases are short sentences that are easy to repeat.

Here are some examples:

- "I've got this."

- "I'm good."
- "Act confident."
- "All I can do is my best."
- "Smile and make friends."

Make sure your catchphrase is something you can believe about yourself. Repeating something farfetched won't do any good. This is not the time to tell yourself that you're the fastest runner on the planet or the smartest kid in the universe.

Whenever you get someone else's mean words stuck in your head, repeat your catchphrase to yourself to drown out their negativity. Every time you do this, you'll empower yourself to feel better.

REFLECTION:

What's a mean name or an insult that replays in your head and causes you to feel bad?

_____

_____

Now create your own catchphrase that you can repeat when something unhelpful replays in your head. You can borrow one of the phrases above if you want, but you might be better off coming up with one in your own words.

THINK BEFORE YOU FEEL

Jayden felt bad about himself because he cared too much about his friends' opinions. He thought if they liked sports, and he didn't, then there must be something wrong with him. He gave them power over how he felt about himself. He started to feel better as soon as he realized he didn't have to be like them in order to be okay.

When someone says something that hurts your feelings, or they suggest that you should change, stop and think before you get caught up in your feelings.

Criticism can hurt! But not all criticism is bad.

Here's the difference:

- A kid who makes fun of your shirt is probably trying to make **themselves** feel better.
- A coach who criticizes how you played the game is probably trying to help **you** become better.

It's important to recognize the difference between helpful and unhelpful criticism. Think about this before you react to someone who criticizes you.

Otherwise, you may get upset over something someone says for no good reason! If you do, you give that person power over you.

Here are some questions to ask yourself the next time you get a little criticism:

- Is this person trying to help me become better? Or are they trying to make themselves feel better?
- Do I value this person's opinion?
- What can I learn from what this person is saying?

Even helpful criticism can still hurt! For instance, let's say that your dad says you aren't doing a good job with your chores. Or a teacher says you need to work harder on your assignments. Things like this can be tough to hear.

Take a deep breath before you reply. Hit pause for a minute or two.

That little pause can prevent you from saying something that will land you in trouble. It can give your brain a few seconds to calm down so you can respond in a helpful way. This is where you need to act brave! We'll talk about that next.

REFLECTION:

Think back to a time when someone else's words hurt you. Do you think that person was trying to make themselves feel better? Or were they really trying to help you improve?

_____

_____

ACT BRAVE

USE EMPOWERING WORDS

Before Jayden could really feel better about himself, he had to change his language. As long as he blamed his friends for *making him* feel bad, he was never going to move on. He needed to empower himself by using different words.

This is because the words you use have a lot of power. And everyday language can give people power over you. Fortunately, once you recognize this, you can find new words.

Here are some phrases that give other people power over you:

MAKES ME: My friend MAKES ME feel bad about myself!

- It might be true that you feel bad because of your friend's behavior sometimes. But she doesn't force you to feel bad about yourself. It's up to you to be in control of how you feel about yourself. You can feel good about yourself no matter what anyone says.

DRIVES ME: My little brother DRIVES ME nuts.

- You might find a younger sibling annoying. But he's not forcing you to feel upset. You are in control of how you respond to other people. You can decide to walk away or do something different without allowing him to upset you.

HAVE TO: I HAVE TO do my homework right now.

- Maybe your parents say it's time to do your homework. Of course, if you don't listen to them, there will probably be a consequence. But they aren't forcing you to move your pencil on the page. It's a choice you are making—because you want to do the right thing (or you want to avoid getting in trouble).

When you find yourself using those phrases, empower yourself with different language. Use words that show you are in control of how you think, feel, and behave no matter what the people around you are doing.

Change your sentences to show that you're keeping your power. Here are some examples of things you can say instead:

- I don't like it when my friend brags and puts me down.
- I feel frustrated when my little brother tries to annoy me.
- I am choosing to do my homework now.

It's hard to break the habit of giving away your power if you've been doing it for a long time. So each time you catch yourself using words that give other people power over you, repeat them in a way that empowers you. With practice, it will be much easier!

REFLECTION:

What's a sentence you use that gives people power over you?

_____

_____

How can you change that sentence to empower yourself?

_____

_____

Traps to Avoid

Some people confuse empowering themselves with trying to be powerful over other people. But bullying someone else, intimidating someone, or being mean are not ways to keep your power! In fact, those kinds of behaviors show that those people lack power over their own feelings. Don't try to gain power over other people in a harmful way.

Sometimes kids feel like they have no power at all. They might think things like, "I'm just a kid. I don't matter." But the truth is that kids are very powerful! Like all humans, they have the power to make meaningful changes, starting in their own lives.

Sadly, there may be times that you don't give your power to someone else—they just steal it. Let's say someone threatens to post embarrassing pictures of you online if you don't do what they tell you to do. So you do the stuff they say just because you don't want them to post those pictures.

Or maybe a kid threatens to beat you up if you don't hand over your lunch money. So you give them your money to avoid getting hurt.

This doesn't mean you gave that kid power over you, though. It means that person abused their power by taking something from you. Don't be hard on yourself if someone steals your power. Things like this are not your fault!

If someone has been stealing your power, you might need help from a trusted adult. Remember those adults we identified in the introduction that you said you could talk to? This might be a good time to reach out to one of them and talk about how someone abused their power.

QUICK TIPS

Strong kids know they need to keep all their power, not give it away. So they empower themselves to remain in control of how they think, feel, and act. When you notice you're giving away your power, remember the exercises that will help you think big, feel good, and act brave.

THINK BIG: Create a catchphrase you can repeat to yourself to drown out your negative thoughts.

Feel GOOD: Think before you feel. Decide whether someone's comments are meant to make them feel better or to help you do better.

ACT BRAVE: Change the words you use to show that you are in control of how you think, feel, and behave.

3

They Adapt to Change

Nala felt angry when she walked into her new school. She knew she was going to hate it. At her old school, the teachers were nice, she had a lot of friends, and she was one of the best saxophone players in the band.

But her parents had decided to move across town to a "nicer" house, so Nala had to switch schools. If you asked her, the new house wasn't even that great. She liked her old bedroom, her old neighborhood, and even her old bus stop much better.

On the first day at the new school, Nala reported to the office like she had been told.

The guidance counselor said, "As a new student, you've been assigned a buddy. Your buddy will teach you how to go through the lunch line, show you how to find your classes, and make sure you have everything you need to be comfortable at our school. Have a seat. Your buddy will be here to pick you up in a few minutes."

Nala tried not to roll her eyes.

She sat down and waited for her "buddy" to come get her. Pretty soon a girl sat down across from her and said, "I'm waiting to see the nurse. Are you?"

Nala said, "Nope. I'm just waiting for my babysitter . . . or buddy . . . or whatever you call them."

The other girl laughed and said, "You must be a new kid."

Nala just ignored her. She thought staying silent was kinder than telling Captain Obvious that of course she was new. Was everyone at this school going to be so annoying?

A minute later, a girl with a big grin practically skipped into the room. "Hi, I'm Victoria! I'm your buddy," she said. "I'll tell you everything you need to know about our school—especially what days you'll want to avoid pizza in the cafeteria. I mean pizza sounds good, but it definitely doesn't taste good."

As Nala followed Victoria toward the lockers, she

could only think, "What school is so bad that they can't make decent pizza?"

Victoria waited as Nala put her backpack inside her locker. Then Victoria guided her to her homeroom, chatting all the way. Nala tuned her out. And within two minutes of stepping into her homeroom, she could tell that none of the kids in this class would be her new friends. She found her seat and pulled out a book. She wasn't really reading it, though. She was just pretending to read so that no one would talk to her! She didn't feel like answering anyone's questions about who she was or where she was from.

Nala just wanted to get through the day so she could call her real friends later and tell them about the longest, worst day of her life.

Check Yourself

Change can be tough. And sometimes there's not a lot you can do about it. You might find yourself with a new stepfamily. You might have a new teacher or coach with different rules. It's natural to want to resist change at first. But trying to stay the same when the world around you is changing can only make things worse.

How much trouble do you have dealing with

change? Check out the sentences below. How many of these statements sound like you?

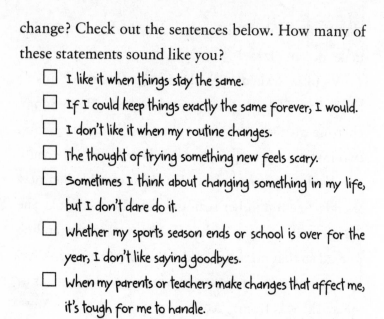

- ☐ I like it when things stay the same.
- ☐ If I could keep things exactly the same forever, I would.
- ☐ I don't like it when my routine changes.
- ☐ The thought of trying something new feels scary.
- ☐ Sometimes I think about changing something in my life, but I don't dare do it.
- ☐ Whether my sports season ends or school is over for the year, I don't like saying goodbyes.
- ☐ When my parents or teachers make changes that affect me, it's tough for me to handle.

It's true that change can be hard, but we also grow from trying different things. If you have a hard time accepting change, there are things you can do to be more flexible.

We're not talking about the type of flexibility that will help you touch your toes. We're talking about being open to meeting new people and trying new experiences. In this chapter we'll discuss why it's hard to deal with change, and—more important—we will find out how to make change a little easier.

But first, let's get back to Nala and her new school. . . .

Closer Look

Nala had no interest in trying to make friends at her new school. She didn't care about her classes. She didn't like her teachers. She figured the only time she would have any fun was when she got to see her old friends on the weekends.

So for the first couple of weeks, Nala trudged through the school day barely looking up. She didn't make eye contact with anyone. She didn't want teachers to call on her in class. She didn't even want to start getting used to the new school.

When her parents asked about her day, she always gave the same answer: "Terrible!"

She wanted them to know that they'd made a mistake. This new house wasn't better! This new neighborhood was awful! And her new school was way worse! All Nala wanted was to go back to the way things used to be.

Even if you've never had to change schools, you can probably relate to Nala's experience. Maybe you didn't want to move on to the next grade one year. Or maybe you weren't happy when you learned you were going to have a new sibling.

Things in your life may have changed naturally, like you grew taller or the weather got colder when the seasons changed. Or maybe someone else changed things for you—like your parents got divorced. Perhaps you even decided to change yourself by switching the sport or the instrument you play.

Whatever change you had to face, you probably struggled to get used to it at first.

Here is why change is so hard:

CHANGE IS SCARY.

You don't know what's going to happen when things change. Will life get better? Will things get worse? If only you could know the ending when you're at the beginning.

CHANGE IS UNCOMFORTABLE.

Having a new routine, following new rules, or being in a new place feels uncomfortable. Nothing is easy or automatic.

CHANGE CAN BE SAD.

Doing something new often means you are leaving something behind. You might feel sad about the memories you won't have with you in the next part of your life.

REFLECTION:

Think about a change in your life that was hard. How did you feel at that time?

_____

_____

PROOF POSITIVE

Nala spent most of her days collecting evidence to prove her new school wasn't as good as her old school. Every night, she shared whatever proof she had with her parents.

Nala secretly hoped that she could convince her parents to move back to her old neighborhood. If they saw how much she hated the new setup, maybe they'd be open to going back.

But that didn't happen. The more she tried to tell them that her new school was awful, the more they tried to convince her to give it a fair chance. And this just made Nala hate her new school even more!

There may have been a time when you also only focused on all the bad things that came along with a change in your life. You, too, were missing the other side of the story.

Here are some ways that change can actually be good:

TRYING NEW THINGS CAN BE EXCITING!

You can try out a new hobby. You can even learn a new language. Doing new things can add spice to your life.

DOING SOMETHING DIFFERENT TEACHES YOU A LOT.

You can learn a lot about yourself, other people, and the world when you are dealing with a new situation.

YOU'LL MEET NEW PEOPLE.

You can meet a lot of cool new people if you are open to new experiences.

IT MIGHT MAKE YOUR LIFE BETTER.

You might think life is good now. But there's always a chance that it can be even better when you try something new.

A lot of good can come from adapting to changes in your life. But sometimes that is easier said than done.

Fortunately, there are some exercises that can help you get more comfortable with change.

HOW DID NALA GROW STRONGER?

Nala visited her old friends after school and on the weekends. But after a few weeks, that wasn't as fun as it used to be. Her friends would talk about things that happened in their school, like the weird thing the teacher did or the fight that almost broke out in the cafeteria that day, and Nala felt left out. She wasn't part of their inside jokes anymore. She felt lonelier than ever.

Then one day the band teacher at her new school came up to her. He said he was looking for a saxophone player for an after-school band he had started. He'd heard she was good.

Nala was really surprised. "How did you hear that?" she asked. It turned out that his son went to Nala's old school. And he had heard her play in the spring concert last year.

Nala smiled. She liked being noticed. Feeling happier than she had in weeks, she said, "I'll think about it!"

But she didn't really have to think about it. She missed playing her saxophone, and she wanted to do something after school. She had been so bored lately! The next day she told the band teacher to count her in.

This after-school band was a lot different than what she was used to. The instruments were different, for one thing, and the kids seemed to take themselves less seriously than the kids in her old band class. *Maybe they had more fun, though?* This band didn't just practice the same songs over and over. The teacher encouraged the kids to come up with their own ideas for songs they wanted to play.

Finally Nala asked, "What exactly are we practicing for?"

Her teacher said, "For fun . . ."

Nala said, "Right, I get it. But really, when is there a concert or a performance?"

Her teacher explained, "There isn't one. We're just making music because we all love music!"

At first Nala felt uncomfortable with this idea. How was she supposed to know if she was getting better? Who would appreciate the hard work she put in?

Wouldn't her parents want to hear what she was doing?

But she still looked forward to these after-school band meetings (she didn't even call them practice anymore), and that helped her feel a little better. And once Nala started having fun with the band, she had to admit that school became a little better, too.

She met a few kids who weren't so bad—mostly the ones who came to the band meetings. And a few of the teachers were okay too. The cafeteria food was even a little better than she'd thought at first (except for the pizza).

Nala realized something. If she kept thinking her new school would be awful, then she would be right! If she kept thinking these new kids were never going to be her friends, she would be right about that, too. The more negative thoughts she had, the more she would act in a way that made those thoughts come true.

She had to think more positive thoughts if she wanted to feel better! And she had to act brave if she was going to make good things happen. She needed to be more open to the idea that change could be good. And while her new school was different, it didn't have to be worse.

Exercises

THINK**BIG**

LOOK FOR THE SILVER LINING

Before Nala could feel better about her new school, she had to think differently. She had to be willing to see that her new school had some good points. Even though it was tough for her to adjust to all the changes, she had to stop expecting everything to be terrible. She had to look for the silver lining.

There's an old saying: "Every cloud has a silver lining." This means that even dark clouds have a bright side! After all, a dark cloud brings rain, which might ruin your outdoor plans. But those same rain clouds water the plants so you can have food to eat. And they give you water to drink.

This can be true with the things you face every day. No matter how rough something feels, there's often something good that can come out of it. You just have to think big if you want to find the silver lining.

Here are some examples:

SITUATION: I didn't make the team.

- **Silver lining:** I'll have more time to try something else I've wanted to do!

SITUATION: There's a power outage.

- **Silver lining:** I can play card games with my family!

SITUATION: My parents can't afford to send me to summer camp.

- **Silver lining:** I'll find fun stuff to do at home with my friends!

REFLECTION:

Think about a rough situation you've faced in the past (or something you are going through right now). Think about how something good could come out of something that seems bad. Here are some questions to consider:

Is there a lesson you could learn from this?

_____

_____

Is there a way you could get better because of this?

_____

_____

_____

Feel GOOD

NAME YOUR FEELINGS

Nala felt better when she accepted her emotions. She had a lot of feelings—disappointment, sadness, anxiety, anger, and loneliness. And she tried to hide all those feelings by pretending she hated everything!

But experts have discovered an interesting fact. Sometimes, just naming your feelings can take a lot of the sting out of them. Saying, "I'm really scared," or "I'm nervous right now," might help you feel a little bit better. Labeling those emotions in your head might be all it takes.

Most of us don't spend much time thinking about how we feel, however. We tend to put more energy into pushing those emotions away (even fighting them). In fact, many people—even adults—have trouble listing more than a couple of feeling words.

Here are some feeling words to help you get started:
- Happy
- Silly
- Excited
- Comfortable

- Jealous
- Embarrassed
- Grumpy
- Sad
- Helpless
- Frightened

The next time you're struggling emotionally or you're having a hard time adjusting to change, label the emotions you're feeling. You might start to feel better right away.

Of course, you usually feel more than one thing at a time. You may be excited *and* nervous about going to the dance. Or maybe you're sad *and* embarrassed that you failed a test. But naming all these feelings can help you make a little more sense of what may feel like a big jumbled mess.

You might find that naming your feelings helps you feel better. You might even find it's helpful to write them down or share them with someone you trust.

REFLECTION:

Take a minute and think about how you are feeling right now as you read this. Name your feeling.

_____

_____

ACT BRAVE

PRACTICE "STEPS" TO PROBLEM-SOLVING

When Nala started her new school, she was faced with a few problems. She missed her old friends, she didn't know anyone at her new school, and she wasn't happy. She had to make some changes if she wanted to feel better. And one big change came when the band teacher invited her to join the after-school group.

If she had done a little problem-solving before this, she may have been able to make herself better all on her own. She could have found the band (or another activity) before the teacher even asked her to join.

When you are faced with a change, you might not know what to do. You could be tempted to do what Nala did at first—nothing at all. For example, if you don't know how to do your schoolwork, you might just not do it (instead of reaching out for help).

But when you're faced with a change, it's important to act bravely! Face your problems head on! The best way to solve a problem is by creating a great plan.

The "STEPS" method is one of the best ways to make a plan to deal with a problem.

Here's what STEPS stands for:

- **S**ay what the problem is.
- **T**hink of five potential solutions.
- **E**valuate why each solution might be good or bad.
- **P**ick one.
- **S**ee if it works.

Here's an example of how STEPS can work to solve a problem:

SAY WHAT THE PROBLEM IS.

I've been staring at my math homework for twenty minutes. I don't know what I'm supposed to do.

THINK OF FIVE POTENTIAL SOLUTIONS.
1. I could ask one of my parents to help me.
2. I could tell my parents I don't have any homework.
3. I could call a friend for help.
4. I could ask my teacher for help tomorrow.
5. I could say I lost my paper.

EVALUATE WHY EACH SOLUTION MIGHT BE GOOD OR BAD.
1. I could ask one of my parents to help me.

This might be good because I could get it done to-night!

This might be bad because my parents don't always understand what my teacher wants me to do.

2. **I could tell my parents I don't have any homework.**

This might be good because I can play video games instead of staring at my paper.

This might be bad because I'll get in trouble for lying. And my work still won't get done!

3. **I could call a friend for help.**

This might be good because I could get it done to-night!

This might be bad because my friend might not know how to help me either.

4. **I could ask my teacher for help tomorrow.**

This might be good because my teacher will know how to help me.

This might be bad because I won't have it done be-fore class.

5. **I could say I lost my paper.**

This might be good because it will get me out of doing my work tonight.

This might be bad because I might get in trouble for lying. And I'll still have to do the work!

PICK ONE.

I will call a friend for help.

SEE IF IT WORKS.

My friend wasn't home. So I'll try asking Dad for help instead.

There are many different ways to solve any problem. But before you jump in and try to fix something, take a minute to think about your options. It's okay to think of some creative solutions. It's called brainstorming. Even if they seem a little farfetched, write your ideas down. Coming up with more ideas will help you arrive at the best solution in the end.

If you practice, you can get better at solving problems. When you are more confident, then you will adapt to changes better!

REFLECTION:

What's a problem you're having in your life right now? Use the STEPS to problem-solving to address it.

Say what the problem is.

_____

_____

THINK OF FIVE POTENTIAL SOLUTIONS.

1. _____
   _____

2. _____
   _____

3. _____
   _____

4. _____
   _____

5. _____
   _____

EVALUATE WHY EACH SOLUTION MIGHT BE GOOD
OR BAD.

1. _____
   _____

2. _____
   _____

3. _____
   _____

4. _____
   _____

5. _____
   _____

Traps to Avoid

Sometimes you choose to make changes in your life. But there will be other times when you don't get to choose. Your parents might move, your teacher might retire, or your grandmother might get too sick to live at home.

Big changes that you don't have control over can be the toughest to handle (we'll talk more about that in Chapter 4). Practice dealing with life's smaller changes first. That way, you will be better prepared to handle the big changes when they arrive.

Be careful that you don't start thinking you can't handle change, or that things were better before they changed. If you do, go back to Chapter 1 and work on replacing those BLUE thoughts with _true_ thoughts!

If you're feeling really stuck, and you just don't think you're going to be okay, then talk to someone. Tell an adult or a trusted friend how you are feeling. You might just need a little help to see that things aren't as bad as you think.

QUICK TIPS

Strong kids embrace the changes in their lives. They work on adapting to the things going on around them instead of resisting them. The next time you're struggling to adjust to change, focus on these exercises that will help you think big, feel good, and act brave!

THINK BIG: In every bad situation, there might be a bright side. Look for the silver lining!

Feel GOOD: Name your feelings. It will make good feelings stand out, and it will take the sting out of bad ones.

ACT BRAVE: Tackle your problems head on by practicing the STEPS to problem-solving.

4

They Focus on Things They Have Control Over

Logan's language arts assignment was to write a speech about someone he admired. His teacher said the class could write about a celebrity, a historical figure, or even someone they knew in real life.

All the kids began brainstorming people they might pick—mostly athletes, singers, rappers, and YouTubers. But Logan knew right away who his speech was going to be about.

His grandmother was the person he admired most in life, and he knew he would have no trouble writing a two-page speech about her. He was sure the list of good things about her could be a mile long if he had enough time to write that much.

The first draft of the speech wasn't due for a few days, but Logan was so excited to write it that he got it done that night.

He handed it to his mom to read. When she was done, she said, "I think you should share this with Gram! She's going to love that you picked her for your speech. I'm proud of you for picking her, too. She's someone special, and we are lucky to have her in our lives."

Logan beamed with pride! He said, "I'll share it with her when it's all done, but I want my teacher to edit it first. I want to make sure it's perfect before Gram reads it!"

He turned the paper in to his teacher the next day. It took him a few days to correct it. When he passed it back to Logan, it had some suggestions about how he could make it even better. Written at the top of the paper was a note that said, "Give a little more background information about your grandmother. Tell us when you first realized she was special. Give some more examples of the things you like about her."

Logan made the changes his teacher suggested, and he couldn't wait to share it with Gram!

But the next day at school, Logan's teacher started talking about how to deliver a good speech. He said, "Stand up straight and try not to fidget—that's distracting. You can look at your notes, but don't read from your paper. Look up at your audience when you're speaking to them."

Hearing those words reminded Logan that this wasn't just a paper he was writing. It was a speech he was going to have to give! The thought of standing in front of the entire class made his palms sweaty. Suddenly he was a lot less excited about this assignment.

His mind raced.

"I hate it when everyone stares at me. What if they think I sound dumb? What if my face turns red and everyone laughs? I don't want to do this!"

Right about then, Logan snapped back to reality. He heard his teacher say, "I know some of you are feeling a bit nervous about giving a speech. But this is a great time to practice your public speaking skills. I'm going to help you, and your classmates are going to be cheering you on. I know all of you can do this!"

Logan wasn't convinced that he could do it, though. He was too shy to even raise his hand in class when he knew an answer. How on earth could he give his presentation in front of everyone?

In one week, the class had to deliver their speeches. That meant he had seven days to imagine all the things that could go wrong. It also meant he had plenty of time to try to figure out how to get out of doing this assignment.

Check Yourself

It's good to focus on things you can control, like how much effort you put into a project or how you treat other people. But sometimes we waste energy on stuff we can't control, like worrying about what *other* kids choose to do. Take a look at these next sentences. How many of them sound like you?

- ☐ I'm always trying to make sure nothing bad **ever** happens.
- ☐ I never ask for help. I want to do everything myself!
- ☐ I don't really like being on a team. Other people don't do their jobs!
- ☐ I don't trust many people—not even my friends.
- ☐ I try to make other people change.
- ☐ I get mad when people don't do things my way!
- ☐ I blame myself for things that probably aren't even my fault.

Do any of these sound familiar? If so, you might be wasting energy on situations you can't control. Fortunately, you can learn how to stop worrying about things like this! You can put your energy into stuff you actually can control. In this chapter, we'll talk about how to figure out what you can control and what you can't. We'll make sure you're putting your energy into the right place!

But first, let's get back to Logan and his speech. . . .

Closer Look

Logan was still worried about whether his classmates would like his speech. He wanted everyone to think he was smart and to appreciate his stories about Gram. But he was afraid the other kids would laugh at him if his speech wasn't good enough.

He was so worried about what everyone was going to think of his speech that he didn't make time to memorize what he was going to say. Logan forgot about the one thing he could control—how he gave his speech! He certainly couldn't control whether the class liked it.

It's easy to do what Logan did and put all your energy in the wrong place. He couldn't control other people—and neither can you. You can only control how *you* act!

Here are some more examples of the difference between what you can control and what you can't control:

SITUATION: Someone makes fun of you.

- What you can control: how you respond to them
- What you can't control: what they think of you

87

SITUATION: You have a big test tomorrow.

- **What you can control:** how long and hard you study
- **What you can't control:** how hard the test is

SITUATION: You're having a birthday party.

- **What you can control:** who you invite and where the party is held
- **What you can't control:** how many people show up

SITUATION: You have basketball tryouts next week.

- **What you can control:** how much you practice and how much effort you put in
- **What you can't control:** whether you get picked for the team

SITUATION: You're getting ready to run a race.

- **What you can control:** whether you do your best
- **What you can't control:** how fast the other kids run

SITUATION: You're going to summer camp.

- **What you can control:** how kindly you treat the other campers
- **What you can't control:** whether people like you

We all waste time and energy on things we have zero control over. And while it may not seem like a big deal, it can create some big problems for you. Up next, we'll talk about why it's so important to stop this behavior.

REFLECTION:

What's an example of a time when you focused on something you couldn't control?

_____

_____

What could you have focused on instead?

_____

_____

PROOF POSITIVE

The big day for the speech finally arrived and Logan felt more nervous than ever! He had spent the last week imagining how his classmates would react to his presentation. He pictured how great it would be if he got a standing ovation. But then he also imagined how embarrassing it would be if everyone laughed at him.

He was still mostly thinking about what his

classmates might think. He wasn't putting much thought into what he was actually going to say.

Logan figured he could just speak off the top of his head. After all, he was talking about his grandmother. He didn't need any notes. He knew Gram better than anyone!

Logan's teacher asked, "Who wants to give their speech first?"

One kid raised his hand and said, "Me! I'll get mine over with now."

Logan started listening to this kid's speech, but he tuned out pretty quickly. He was too nervous to focus.

Several more kids took their turns giving speeches. But when no one else volunteered to go next, the teacher said, "Okay, I'm just going to pick someone then. Logan, you're up."

Logan felt dizzy as he walked up to the front of the class. His heart pounded so hard he thought it might fly out of his chest. His palms were sweaty. He could feel his face turning red.

He took a deep breath and stared at his classmates. He had absolutely no idea what to say. His mind drew a complete blank!

He just stood there, fumbling for something to say. His teacher tried to help him out. "Start by telling us a bit about who your grandmother is, Logan."

"Okay," Logan said.

He recited a few facts about what kind of work his grandmother used to do and where she grew up. But he quickly ran out of words again.

His teacher gave another prompt. "Tell us a bit about why you admire her so much, Logan."

Logan shared a few short examples of things he thought made his grandmother amazing. But then he just rushed to his seat and put his head in his hands. He knew he'd messed up. He hadn't said all the things he wanted to say. And he definitely didn't get a standing ovation.

Maybe you can recall a time when you worried about the wrong things. It happens to all of us, of course. And, like Logan, you may have experienced some disappointment because you focused on things you had no control over.

Here are some reasons you should focus only on what you can control:

- **You'll keep your worries in check.**
  Your worries can get out of hand if you start worrying about things you can't control (whether it's going to rain tomorrow, whether your friend is going to show up for your party, etc.).

- **You'll save your energy for problems you can fix.**
  You need energy to solve problems. You don't want to waste it on things you can't change.
- **You'll be more pleased with yourself.**
  When you focus on doing your best (instead of beating everyone else), you will feel better about yourself.
- **You'll get along better with other people.**
  When you try to force other people to act the way you want them to, you're probably going to get in a lot of arguments!

Putting all your energy into the things you have control over will help you do your best—and feel your best. Of course, it's easy to say and harder to do. But next we'll go through some exercises that can help you stay focused on the stuff you can control.

REFLECTION:

What's an example of a time when you stayed focused on something you had control over?

_____

_____

_____

HOW DID LOGAN GROW STRONGER?

Logan felt embarrassed about the speech he gave (or attempted to give). He thought he let his grandmother down because he didn't share all the stories he wanted to tell about her. He let himself down, too, because he knew he could have done better.

A couple weeks later, Logan's teacher assigned another presentation. Logan thought, "Here we go again!"

He felt nervous all over. He didn't want to mess up like he did the first time.

So he worked hard writing his speech! And this time he practiced delivering it. He stood in front of the mirror every day for a week, and he went over all the things he wanted to say. He even used notecards to help him remember facts and stories.

He rehearsed how he would stand, how he would look at the audience, and even the times when he would pause. Every once in a while, he thought things like, "What if no one claps?" or, "What if they laugh at me?"

But when those thoughts crept into his brain, he just

reminded himself, "Focus on doing your best!"

He felt nervous when the big day to deliver the second speech finally arrived. But when the teacher called on him to go next, Logan noticed that his nerves actually went down a little. He felt way better than last time, for sure!

He walked up to the front of the class and looked at the audience—just like he had been practicing in his room. He delivered the best speech he could give. When he was done, he took his seat and smiled. He felt so

proud of himself that he barely noticed how loudly everyone was clapping for him!

How did Logan pull it off? This time he focused on doing his best, not what the other kids would think. And that's just what he did!

Exercises

THINK BIG

CHANGE THE CHANNEL

Whenever Logan started imagining all the horrible things that could go wrong during his speech, he needed to replace those thoughts. Thinking about people laughing at him wasn't doing any good. It was better to use that time and energy to rehearse.

So whenever he began worrying about things he had no control over, he listened to music for a few minutes. Listening to his favorite songs helped him think about happier things. And that helped calm his nerves about giving the speech.

He also created a catchphrase (like we talked about in Chapter 2). And it helped silence his negative thoughts when he practiced.

You can probably relate to Logan's experience on

some level. Have you had something stuck in your head that you just couldn't get rid of? Maybe it was something kind of fun, like a funny commercial you can't stop thinking about. Or maybe it was something that bothered you and put you in a bad mood—like a mean thing someone said to you at school.

You might replay it in your head, almost like you're watching the same scene in a movie over and over again. Or it might feel like the same song is just stuck on repeat in your brain.

When you have something stuck in your head that causes you to feel bad, you need to "change the channel." Treat your brain like a TV. Put it on a different station. Turn it to something that helps you feel better.

How can you do this? Well, telling yourself, "Don't think about that!" usually doesn't work. In fact, the more you tell yourself *not* to think about something, the more it usually pops into your head.

So how do you turn your brain to a better channel? Here is the secret. Are you ready?

Do something that makes you forget what you were thinking about. It's that simple.

Design a fun challenge for yourself that takes a little brainpower. It can be anything. It can even be silly things like:

- Trying to find all the red cards in a deck within thirty seconds
- Trying to recite the alphabet backward
- Trying to write your name with the opposite hand than you usually write with

Or go shoot some baskets in the driveway or at the park. Moving around and playing something you enjoy will distract your brain. And when your brain is distracted from the bad stuff, then the happier stuff will have room to sneak in!

Here are some other things you might do to change the channel:

- Listen to or play some music
- Exercise
- Do some artwork
- Read a good book
- Organize or decorate your room
- Play a game with your siblings
- Call a friend and talk (just don't talk about the thing you're trying to forget)

REFLECTION:

What's a fun challenge you could create for yourself to change the channel in your brain the next time you're struggling to get your mind off something that upsets you?

_____

_____

Create your own list of at least five things you can do to change the channel in your brain. Keep the list handy. The next time you get something stuck in your head, pick something from the list. And do it!

1. _____

2. _____

3. _____

4. _____

5. _____

Feel GOOD

SCHEDULE TIME TO WORRY

When Logan was worried about how other kids in the class would react to his speech, he could have scheduled time to worry.

That sounds ridiculous, right? We want to worry less. So why would we purposely set aside time to worry?

Well, experts found that people who plan to worry actually end up worrying less! Rather than worry all day long, they just worry for a little while. Then they move on with their day.

If you worry a lot, find a regular time to worry every day. Just make sure you only worry for a few minutes. This can help you get control over your brain—and stop you from focusing on things you have no control over.

You might make the bus stop your "worry time and place." While you wait for the bus, think about all the bad things you fear happening. Then, when you get on the bus, tell yourself, "It's time to stop worrying!"

If you catch yourself worrying at any time other than at the bus stop, remind yourself it's not time to worry. You will have to wait until tomorrow's bus stop for that. Until then, you can just concentrate on having the best day possible.

Of course, your worry time doesn't have to be at the bus stop. It can be anywhere.

Think about a time that might be good for you to worry. Just remember that you might not want to pick right before you go to bed. If you worry before bed, it might be tougher to get to sleep. And you don't want that!

ACT BRAVE

CHARGE YOUR BATTERIES

When Logan gave his first speech, he was mentally exhausted. He had spent so much time worrying about what was going to happen that he didn't do anything fun or relaxing all week. His batteries were drained! That made it impossible for him to perform at his best.

Like Logan, there may be times in your life when your batteries run out of juice. We're not talking about the kind of batteries you put in your TV remote, though. We're talking about your personal energy level.

Have you ever thought about that? You probably don't think twice about charging your electronics, do you? You know that the battery wears down, and you need to plug in your phone, tablet, or computer if you want to use them.

Just like your electronics, you need recharging every

once in a while, too. You won't literally run out of battery life. But you will run out of energy and patience if you don't ever take time to chill out.

You can't control all the stressful things you might face in life. But you can control how well you "charge your batteries" to deal with them. The best way to do this is by taking time to do things that relax you.

Here's a list of things that can help charge your batteries:

- Listen to chill music
- Go for a walk
- Relax at the park with a friend
- Take pics of nature
- Take a long, hot bath
- Drink some hot chamomile tea
- Do yoga

It's important to do calming things regularly. Try for at least thirty minutes a day. When your batteries are fully charged, you'll have more energy to focus on the things you have control over.

REFLECTION:

What things can you do at home to charge your batteries?

_____

_____

How can you make time to do those things every single day?

_____

_____

Traps to Avoid

When your mind gets stuck on the same thing over and over, ask yourself, "Is this a problem I can fix?" If so, use the STEPS problem-solving that we talked about in Chapter 3. If it's a problem you can't fix, change the channel in your brain.

There may be times when you get something sort of fun stuck in your head—like you can't stop thinking about that person you have a crush on. But even those "fun" thoughts might distract you from other activities you want and need to do. Sometimes it may be a good idea to change the channel for a little while, even when you're thinking positive thoughts.

At other times, we replay moments in our heads that

just aren't fun. If something really bad happened to you, and you can't stop replaying it in your mind, talk to an adult. A trusted adult can help you create a plan. You might even need to talk to a professional counselor who can help you feel better. Don't be shy about asking for help. Asking for help will make you stronger!

QUICK TIPS

Strong kids focus on things they have control over. When they find themselves worried about something outside of their control, they practice these exercises to help them think big, feel good, and act brave to get back on track.

THINK BIG: Do you have something stuck in your brain that you just can't get out? Change the channel to something better!

Feel GOOD: Schedule time to worry about anything you want. Just don't let yourself worry outside of your worry time. It will help you worry less!

ACT BRAVE: Take time to relax and charge your batteries so you have energy to focus on the things you have control over.

5

They Know When to Say No

Ava was a really nice girl. She was the kind of kid who was friends with all sorts of people. Some of her friends were older kids who played sports. Some of her friends were on the math team. And some of them she met through church.

Adults liked Ava, too. Her teachers, her coaches, and her Sunday school teacher always knew they could count on her if they needed help. Even her neighbor trusted her to feed her cat while she was away.

Ava liked being a helper. She had younger siblings, and she pitched in whenever her parents needed a hand. She helped her little twin sisters get dressed for school.

She helped her brother with his homework. Ava was always happy to be there for others.

Ava loved it when other kids said she was really nice. And it made her proud when adults called her responsible. She was a good kid who prided herself on going the extra mile.

She liked doing favors. She figured that every kind deed she did for people made them like her more—and this made her like herself a little more, too.

But things changed a little the day her friend Mason asked, "Can I borrow your math homework?"

Ava said, "Sure!" (That's pretty much what she always said when anyone asked for something.)

She reached in her backpack and found her paper. "It's not quite done yet. But you can look at what I've done so far," she said.

Mason said, "Okay, I just need it for a minute." He sat down and began copying Ava's answers. Then he said, "Call me tonight when you get the other few problems done too, okay?"

Ava said, "Sure thing!"

As soon as she got home from school, Ava did her chores. (Her mother loved it when she got her chores done before dinner.)

When the family finished eating, Ava sat down to do her homework. When she was done, she remembered Mason. She called him and said, "I have those math answers for you!"

Mason said, "Great! Read them to me, and I'll write them down."

Ava thought nothing more of it—until a couple of days later.

Ava's math teacher asked Ava and Mason to stay after class because she needed to speak with them. So after the bell rang, they both approached the teacher's desk.

She said, "When I graded your papers, I noticed that both of you got the same questions wrong. In fact, you answered every question exactly the same. This makes me wonder if one of you copied off the other one's paper."

Right away, Ava realized what she had done. She had been so eager to help her friend that it never occurred to her that she was helping him cheat!

He had asked if he could borrow her paper so casually. So she said yes—like she always said yes if anyone wanted to borrow something. She never even stopped to consider that she was doing something wrong.

Check Yourself

Being a people-pleaser like Ava can wear you out quickly. Sure, people like the things you do for them. But trying to please people too much can leave you feeling exhausted and empty. Take a look at these sentences. How many of them sound like you?

- ☐ I say sorry a lot.
- ☐ I feel like it's my job to make everyone happy.
- ☐ It really bothers me when anyone is angry at me.
- ☐ If my friends ask for favors, I always say yes (even if I don't want to).
- ☐ I usually pretend to agree with what my friends say (even if I don't really agree).
- ☐ I don't tell anyone when my feelings are hurt.
- ☐ I sometimes volunteer to do things I don't want to do.

Everyone struggles to speak up, say no, or express their opinions once in a while. But be careful! You might end up saying yes to things that do more harm than good. In this chapter, we'll talk about how to know when to say no. We'll also cover how saying no makes you stronger. And we'll discuss the best exercises for learning how to say no.

But first, let's get back to Ava and the cheating incident. . . .

Closer Look

Ava automatically said yes to everything asked of her. She didn't even think about it. But she did notice that the more she said yes, the more people kept asking. Ava helped her friends learn their new cheers. She helped her grandmother do yard work. She rarely had any time for herself. But she never complained—at least not out loud.

Sometimes she secretly felt a little tired, bored, or irritated about doing so many things for others. But she ignored her feelings and kept smiling. She didn't want to appear selfish. And she didn't want people to think she wasn't nice.

Maybe you're sort of like Ava. You agree to do too much stuff for other people. Some of those things might be favors. But favors might not be the only thing you say yes to.

Perhaps you say yes to things that are supposed to be fun because you're afraid to say no. Have you ever agreed to go to someone's house even if you didn't want to? Maybe you thought saying no would hurt their feelings?

Of course you shouldn't say no to everything you don't want to do. If you did that, you would probably never do homework!

So you shouldn't decide what to do based on your feelings alone.

Speaking up, for example, can be quite uncomfortable. But just like saying no, it's important to voice your opinion sometimes. That's something Ava struggled with too. She rarely ever spoke up, even when her feelings were hurt or when she disagreed with someone else.

Speaking up all the time, however, isn't helpful either. There are other times when voicing your opinion can do more harm than good. It's important to learn the right times to speak up.

Think about these scenarios for a minute. Should you speak up or stay quiet?

1. The umpire in your baseball game says, "Strike!" But you are sure it was a ball!

2. You think you deserve a higher grade than the one your teacher gave you.

3. Your friend tells a joke that makes fun of people who are part of another religion.

4. Your friend borrows something but doesn't give it back.

5. The coach takes you out of the game and says you need to pay more attention.

Let's take a look take a look at each of those situations.

1. Your best bet is to stay quiet. It's the umpire's job to make the calls (and they don't always get them right). But speaking up here might get you thrown out of the game!

2. You might ask a respectful question like, "Can you please explain to me how you calculated my grade?" This could help you learn how to get a better grade in the future. But saying, "This isn't fair!" probably won't get you results.

3. Speaking up sends the message that you don't think it's funny to laugh at people because of their beliefs!

4. Speaking up and asking for your stuff back shows that you respect yourself. And you expect others to treat your property with respect.

5. Arguing with the coach isn't a good idea. In the moment, it's best to stay quiet. After the game, you can talk to the coach. You might discover you were making mistakes without even realizing it.

Take some time to consider how you feel about saying no. Do you say yes to things you really don't think you should do? Do you stay quiet sometimes, even though it might be a better idea to say something? Next we'll talk about why speaking up and saying no can be good for you.

REFLECTION:

Think of a time when you said yes to something you didn't want to do. How did you feel?

_____

_____

Now think of a time when you wished you had spoken up but you didn't say anything. What kept you from speaking up?

_____

_____

PROOF POSITIVE

Ava's teacher gave her a zero for allowing Mason to cheat off her paper. She also had to stay after school for detention.

The punishment hurt a little. Knowing she had made such a big mistake hurt a lot! She was disappointed in herself.

The worst part was facing her parents. When she got home that night they sat down at the table with her and had a talk. Her father said, "We taught you to be honest. I'm disappointed you cheated."

Her mother said, "I know you want to be a nice kid,

Ava. But you need to learn to say no to people who ask you to do things that are wrong."

Ava felt terrible! She never wanted to feel this bad again! She knew she needed to stop trying so hard to make other people happy.

Maybe you can relate to Ava's experience somehow. You may have said yes to something you shouldn't have because you didn't want to disappoint someone, or maybe you just didn't know what to say. When someone is looking right at you and expecting you to say yes, it can be tough to turn them down. It might feel awkward or uncomfortable.

But here is why sometimes it's okay to say no, disagree, or speak up:

- **Your guesses aren't always true.**
  You might guess your friend is going to feel crushed if you can't come over today. You might guess your grandfather is going to be mad if you don't help him with a project. But those are just guesses! Your friend might invite another friend over and still have a good time. Your grandfather may have only asked for your help because he thought you were bored. He might be glad you have something else to do. It might be completely okay to say no!

- **You might hurt your relationships.**

  You might think people will like you more when you agree with everything they say. But if you do, other people will never get to know the real you. You don't want someone to like you only because you agree with everything they say. It's okay to disagree sometimes!

- **You'll forget what's important to you.**

  If you are afraid to speak up when you think something's not right, you might make a mistake just like Ava did. Or you might not stand up for your friends when they need your help. Sometimes you have to say no to protect what's important to you.

REFLECTION:

What is a time when you felt proud of yourself for saying no or speaking up?

_____

_____

_____

How did you find the courage to do it?

_____

_____

_____

HOW DID AVA GROW STRONGER?

Ava's parents lectured her about the cheating incident for quite a while. Her father said, "Ava, next time someone asks you to do something that feels uncomfortable, say no!"

Ava nodded. She thought about it for a minute. Then she said, "But I didn't *feel* uncomfortable at the time! I didn't even really think it was a bad idea."

Her mother threw her hands in the air and said, "Because you automatically say yes to everything people ask of you!"

Her dad said, "Ava, before you answer anyone's requests, stop and take a deep breath. Think about your answer before you respond. Pausing for a few seconds will make sure you are only saying yes to the things you really want to do."

Ava agreed to start pausing before she said yes to people. But it was hard!

Her mother knew this would be difficult for Ava. So she assigned her a weird task. She told her to say no to the next three things that friends asked of her. No matter what they asked, she had to decline. This was just for her to practice saying no.

So Ava did it. When her friend asked her to watch a movie, she said no. When another friend asked her if she wanted to trade snacks at lunch, she said no again. And finally, when a friend asked if she wanted to study for a science test together, she said no for the third time.

She reported back to her mother. Her mother asked, "How was it?"

Ava said, "It wasn't as bad as I thought. No one really seemed to mind."

And while it felt a little weird to say no (especially when she wanted to say yes), that experiment was the beginning of her new game plan. From now on, she would take a deep breath, pause, and think before saying yes or no to anything!

Exercises

THINK BIG

GIVE IT THE "GIVE UP" TEST

The more Ava learned to say no, the easier it became. Part of the reason was this: She realized that every time she said yes to one thing, she was also saying no to something (or someone) else.

Thinking about what you're giving up might help you decide when to say yes and when to say no.

Here are some examples:

- When you say yes to going to a friend's house, you might give up time playing with your siblings.
- When you say yes to helping a neighbor do yard work, you might give up time hanging out with your friends.
- When you say yes to watching a movie with your friends, you might give up time you would have been watching your favorite TV show at home.
- When you say yes to joining the art club, you might give up time you could have used to finish your homework.

Before you say yes to something, give it the "give up" test. If you decide you don't want to give something up, then say no. If you decide you don't mind giving the other thing up, then go ahead and say yes. It's that simple!

REFLECTION:

Think about the last time you said yes to something. What did you give up to do that thing?

_____

_____

Feel GOOD

SMELL THE PIZZA

Ava found it helpful to pause and take a deep breath when she was deciding whether to say yes or no to people who asked favors. But she may have benefited even more from learning to "smell the pizza."

This is something that can be especially helpful if you say yes a lot because you're nervous that someone might get upset with you. If your anxiety goes up when you speak up, then "smell the pizza."

Here's how it works:

1. Take a deep breath in through your nose—like you're smelling a delicious piece of pizza.

2. Count to three slowly.

3. Now pretend you're blowing on the pizza—because it's hot

and you can't wait to take a bite! Breathe out through your mouth slowly. Do that three times. It will calm your brain and your body.

Here are some times when you might "smell the pizza":

- **You see a kid being picked on.** You need to boost your courage before you say something.
- **Your friend calls and invites you to her little sister's dance recital.** It sounds really boring, and you don't want to go. You need to feel brave enough to say no.
- **You see a kid sitting all alone at lunch.** You want to suggest to your friends that you invite the kid to join you. But you're a little scared they might not agree.

REFLECTION:

Practice smelling the pizza right now. How do your mind and body feel?

_____

_____

What are some times when you might want to practice smelling the pizza?

_____

_____

ACT BRAVE

DELIVER A POLITE NO

Ava struggled to say no because it felt weird. She wasn't used to saying it. But the more she practiced, the easier it became!

Sometimes it takes courage to turn someone down. You might struggle to find the right words. After all, you wouldn't want to say, "No, I would rather stay home and stare at the wall than hang out with you!"

So how can you say no and still be kind?

Here are some examples of things you might say:

- "No, I'm not able to."

  Sometimes you don't even need to offer a reason. Just say it doesn't work for you.

- "Thank you so much for inviting me, but I've got other plans."

  Your plans may be reading a book by yourself in your room. But that's your business. You don't need to tell anyone what your other plans are.

- "I'll have to check and get back to you."

  Use this if you need a few minutes to think about it. You don't have to tell them what you are checking. Just make sure you get back to the person and say no if you're not going to accept their invitation. (You don't want to leave them hanging, either.)

- "I'm not really feeling up to that today, but thanks for asking."

You don't have to explain any further than this.

REFLECTION:

What's a polite thing to say when you want to turn someone down gently?

_____

_____

_____

Traps to Avoid

There may be times when someone gets upset with you because you say no. Your friend might say you are being mean for not helping her with her homework. Your cousin might stop talking to you for a while because you didn't want to go to his house.

Just remember that it's okay for other people to be mad at you. It doesn't mean you did anything wrong. They just may need a little space to take care of their own feelings.

There will also be times when you aren't sure if you should speak up. It can be hard to make that choice in the moment. And there is a chance you might regret your decision later. You might stay quiet when you should have spoken. Or you might speak your mind when you should have stayed quiet. Just make sure you learn from those mistakes! (We'll talk more about how to learn from your mistakes in Chapter 8.)

QUICK TIPS

Saying no sometimes can help you become a stronger kid. It'll make sure you have the time and energy to put into the things that are most important to you. When you're struggling to say no or speak up, these exercises can help you think big, feel good, and act brave.

THINK BIG : Every time you say yes to something, you say no to something else. So give it the "give up" test to remind yourself what you're saying no to when you say yes to something else.

Feel GOOD : Anytime you need the courage to speak up or say no, "smell the pizza!" It can calm your brain and your body.

ACT BRAVE: If it is difficult for you to say no some-times, then practice it one small step a time. Have some phrases ready that can help you deliver a polite no in a kind way.

They Take Calculated Risks

Carter was so happy! Summer vacation was finally here. He was going to spend the next few months enjoying freedom. No homework! No alarm clocks! And best of all, no teachers! He imagined he would spend his days playing ball and riding his bike with his two best friends, Sean and Liam.

But just two days into vacation, the chain fell off his bike. He tried to fix it, but he couldn't get it back on. He showed his dad. His dad looked at it and said, "You need a new bike. We can put the chain back on, but it's going to fall off again. The frame is bent."

They stood there in the garage staring at the heap of metal that used to be a bike. "Will you buy me a new bike, then?" Carter asked.

His dad looked at him and said, "The reason your bike is falling apart is that you do too many wild stunts. I'm not going to buy you a new one just so you can break it again!"

Carter's heart sunk. What would he do all summer if he didn't have a bike? So he protested, "Dad, that's not fair! I can't help it that my bike is so cheap it bends!"

His father said, "Carter, your bike wasn't cheap. You take too many jumps on your bike even though we tell you not to! If you want a new bike, you'll have to buy your own."

"But I don't have any money!" Carter said.

His father said calmly, "Then maybe it's time you earn some."

Carter stormed out of the garage. There was no way he could earn enough money to buy a new bike!

He calmed down by dinner and started rethinking his options. He asked, "Can I do some extra chores to earn money for a new bike?"

His dad said, "No. Just because you want more money doesn't mean I have to give you more jobs. If you want to earn money, you should start a business. We have a lawn mower. I'm sure there are plenty of people who would pay you to cut their grass this summer."

Carter spent the next few days thinking about it. Could he really start a lawn-mowing business? He didn't even know where to begin. Should he make flyers? Did he need a website? Could he just walk up to his neighbors and ask, "Hey, can I mow your lawn?"

If he got jobs, how much would he charge? What if he missed a patch of grass and someone got mad? He had way more questions than answers.

Carter really wanted a bike! But starting a business? He had no clue what to do next.

 ## Check Yourself

Some people stay away from risks no matter what— even the ones that could help them have a better life. Other people take risks that are way too big. They don't think about the consequences if things don't work out well.

Check out the following sentences. See whether you are more likely to be a risk-dodger or a risky risk-taker:

RISK-DODGER

- [ ] I talk myself out of doing anything that seems a little scary.
- [ ] I think about all the bad things that could happen if I take a risk.
- [ ] I let other people make decisions for me.

☐ I don't like to try new things. I'm too afraid they will turn out badly!

☐ I like to play things as safe as possible!

RISKY RISK-TAKER

☐ If someone dares me to do something, I just do it.

☐ I sometimes get so excited about all the good things that could happen that I never really think about what could go wrong.

☐ I sometimes get in trouble because I do things without thinking.

☐ After I take a risk, I often realize I messed up!

Which one of those sounds more like you? Of course, you might not always be a risk-dodger *or* a risky risk-taker. Sometimes you may be one, and sometimes you might be the other.

For example, you might take big physical risks, but not any other kind of risk. Maybe you do dangerous stunts like Carter, yet you're too shy to take a social risk, like talk to the new kid at school.

In this chapter, we'll talk more about why we take some risks, but we avoid others. Most important, we will learn how to take smart risks! We will call those calculated risks.

But first, let's get back to Carter and his broken bike. . . .

Closer Look

Carter spent the next two weeks *thinking* about a lawn-mowing business. But did he do anything about it? Nope!

Of course, good planning is important. But Carter didn't develop a plan.

He just kept thinking about all the things that could go wrong. He imagined customers getting angry at him. He pictured his friends laughing at him for working while they were playing.

He never worried about the actual business risks, though. He didn't think about the money he needed to buy gas. He didn't think about the fact that he would be using his parents' lawn mower. These are the risks that should have crossed his mind.

Instead, he was mostly worried about the social risks.

Maybe you can relate to Carter. You may have avoided trying something new because you felt afraid.

Here are some examples:

- You didn't ask someone to go to the dance because you were afraid they would say no.

- You didn't try out for the soccer team because you didn't think you'd make the cut.
- You didn't run for student council because you were afraid you would lose.
- You didn't try out the climbing wall at the gym because you were afraid you might fall (even though there were safety ropes).
- You didn't raise your hand in class because you were afraid you might get the answer wrong.

None of these risks will kill you. They might feel scary, but they aren't actually all that risky.

REFLECTION:

What's a risk you avoided because you felt afraid?

_____

_____

On the other hand, you might do the opposite. You may take some risks that are actually dangerous. That was the case with Carter.

He never even thought twice about doing stunts on his bike! He and his friends brought their bikes to the skate park all the time, and they did all kinds of outrageous stuff! They even tried to copy tricks they saw on YouTube.

One time, Carter tried to ride his bike down the stairs at the town library. That earned him a broken wrist!

His mother told him to be more careful, but Carter wasn't scared. He said, "Mom, I think about how many tricks I land! Not how many I miss."

Even if you don't do stunts on your bike, you may be able to relate to Carter's risk-taking. Here are some examples of risky risk-taking:

- You accept dares from friends to get attention.
- You send text messages during class even though your teacher says no phones allowed.
- You do physical stunts even though you sometimes get hurt doing them.
- You watch a movie with your friend that your parents would never allow you to see.

Taking risks without thinking about the consequences can be bad news. You may get in trouble. You may get hurt. Either way, these kinds of risks usually don't end well!

REFLECTION:

When have you taken too big of a risk in life?

_____

_____

What did you learn from it?

_____

_____

_____

PROOF POSITIVE

Carter felt left out every time he saw his friends riding their bikes. Sometimes when he was playing video games with all of them, one friend would say, "Let's ride our bikes to the park!"

Carter would have to remind them he couldn't go.

One of the guys offered to let Carter borrow his little brother's bike. But Carter was too embarrassed to take it. The only thing worse than not having a bike was riding someone's little brother's bike around the block.

He started looking at bikes online, and he found the one he really wanted. It was way nicer than the one he had!

One night after dinner he approached his dad. He

said, "I've been thinking more about that lawn-mowing business. I want to do it! But I don't know how to get started."

His father smiled. Then he said, "You've already waited a few weeks. Most people have already hired someone to cut their grass this summer. But if you try hard, you can probably still find some customers."

They spent the next hour talking about all the things Carter would need to get his business started. They discussed all the calculated risks he would need to take, like asking people to mow their lawns (even though there was a chance they'd say no).

Carter still felt a little nervous after their conversation. But he also felt excited! He just had to keep thinking about that bike whenever he felt anxious. Yes, he would need to work, but it would all be worth it once he got that bike!

Maybe you can understand what Carter was going through. You may have been faced with a risk you had to talk yourself into, but you tried to keep your mind on the reward.

Taking risks can feel scary. Calculating your risk will help. This means thinking about what could go right and what could go wrong. It also means figuring out if there is a way to risk less and still accomplish your goal. After calculating your risk, you might decide it's a risk worth taking, even if you feel nervous about taking it!

Taking calculated risks can help you learn new things, meet new people, and create a more exciting life. You could even make the world a better place one day by taking a calculated risk. After all, we wouldn't have new ideas or inventions if no one ever took a risk.

Here are some more examples of calculated risks you might take during your life:

- Starting a business
- Taking a tough class
- Trying out for a team
- Applying to college
- Changing jobs
- Getting married
- Buying a house
- Asking for a raise or promotion

Many of these risks might feel scary at first. There's no way to know if they are going to work out. But sometimes, these kinds of risks are worth trying!

REFLECTION:

Can you think of some calculated risks that the adults in your life may have taken?

_____

_____

How did they help them get to where they are today?

_____

_____

HOW DID CARTER GROW STRONGER?

Talking about starting the lawn-mowing business was the easy part. _Doing it_ was much scarier!

Carter sat down with his dad. They talked about what could go right and what could go wrong. If he started the business, he might earn enough money to buy that new bike. Then, he could have a lot more fun with his friends. His dad said some other good stuff could happen, too (like he might learn responsibility).

On the other hand, if he didn't start the business, he wouldn't have to worry about his fear of being rejected or embarrassed. But that also meant he wouldn't get a new bike, either. And the rest of his summer vacation

135

probably wouldn't be as fun.

After they discussed all the options, Carter made his decision. He was convinced that this business was a calculated risk that he wanted to take. He was going to do it!

They rehearsed what he would say to people. Together they created flyers. Carter decided he would hand them out to neighbors and to the people from his church.

He still felt nervous about going up to people, though. Before he started passing out the flyers, his father said, "When your fear tries to talk you out of doing it, remember the bike you want to buy. You'll feel braver!"

That's what Carter did when he began handing out the flyers.

One woman said she didn't need her lawn mowed. But she could use some help with her garden. Carter was good with that!

Another man said, "I take care of my own lawn, kid! But I am going away on vacation for a month. If you are as good as you say you are, I'll hire you temporarily." Carter assured him he could get the job done. And he got hired for that yard, too! He was thrilled that he was really getting business.

Of course, some people said, "No, thank you." But being turned down wasn't as bad as he imagined. It really wasn't a big deal at all. There was always someone else to ask.

At this point, Carter was pretty sure that he could get enough jobs to buy his new bike before the summer ended. Asking people to hire him was a risk. But earning enough money to buy that bike made it a risk worth taking.

Exercises

THINK BIG

ARGUE THE OPPOSITE

When Carter felt afraid, he imagined all the things that could go wrong—like people saying no to him or his friends laughing at him. He could have thought bigger by arguing the opposite. That means purposely thinking about all the things that could go right. Maybe he would get hired by plenty of people! And maybe his friends would think he is cool for earning his own money!

That's what happens when we feel afraid. Our brains remind us of all the things that could go wrong. Our brains even exaggerate how likely we are to fail.

Here's an example:

SITUATION: You're thinking about trying out for the talent show. You want to sing a song.

Thoughts that might run through your head:
- "I probably won't make it."
- "I'll just embarrass myself."
- "I probably sound awful."

- "No one likes my singing."
- "I'll probably get so nervous I'll freak out."

When your brain starts imagining all the things that could go wrong, argue the opposite!

Think about all the things that might go right, like this:
- "I probably won't make it." >>> "I might get picked!"
- "I'll just embarrass myself." >>> "People might be proud of me."
- "I probably sound awful." >>> "I might sound great!"
- "No one likes my singing." >>> "The judges might like my performance!"
- "I'll probably get so nervous I'll freak out." >>> "I'm confident that I can give my best performance!"

Of course, you don't have to think everything will always go perfectly. That wouldn't be helpful, either. The goal is to help balance out the bad thoughts with the good thoughts, because the truth is somewhere in the middle.

More realistic thoughts about the talent show might be, "There's no guarantee I'll make it. But I can try my hardest! I know I'll have fun and do my best."

This could also be a helpful time to replace BLUE thoughts with true thoughts (like we talked about in Chapter 1). But you might decide you like to argue the opposite better. Either exercise can be helpful in combating those negative thoughts!

REFLECTION:

Think of a time when your brain focused on everything that could go wrong. What thoughts were running through your head?

_____

_____

Now argue the opposite!

_____

_____

Now look at both sides of the argument. What's a more realistic thought?

_____

_____

Feel GOOD

TEST YOUR "ANXIETY ALARM"

Carter was scared to start his business. But his anxiety was a false alarm. Asking a neighbor or someone he knew from church to cut their grass wasn't dangerous. He was going to approach people he knew, and his dad would help him. His body and his mind reacted as though it were a life-or-death situation, though!

He didn't have any alarm bells go off when he did bike stunts, did he? And those really were dangerous!

Some risks are supposed to feel scary. The thought of jumping off a cliff should make you afraid. If you were standing on the edge of a cliff, your heart would probably race. You would probably get a knot in your stomach, too. This is your body's way of telling you, "Don't do this!"

Your anxiety is trying to keep you safe by sounding an alarm. (Remember how we talked about times when your feelings can be a friend or enemy in Chapter 1? Your anxiety is your friend when it warns you about something that might be dangerous.)

But there are times when your anxiety alarm bell is a little faulty. It might send your body into panic mode when you're not actually in any danger.

Your heart might beat fast when you try to strike up a conversation with that person you like. Or you might get butterflies in your stomach when you step up to the plate in a baseball game.

In those cases, a little anxiety may actually give you the energy you need to do your best. But too much anxiety might make you think that what you're about to do is a bad idea. Your body might react like you are in a life-or-death situation when clearly you aren't.

When this happens, you might be tempted to become a risk-dodger.

When something *feels* really scary, it's important to take a minute and *think*. Ask yourself if this is a real anxiety alarm or a false alarm.

Here are some examples of times when your anxiety alarm bell might ring:

- You're sitting on the couch when you suddenly smell smoke!—Real alarm
- You're sitting on the couch watching a scary movie.—False alarm
- You're out for a walk and you come across a huge barking dog that looks mean!—Real alarm
- You're out for a walk and a loud, barking Chihuahua startles you.—False alarm
- You're getting ready for school and a stranger starts pounding on your door!—Real alarm
- You're getting ready for school and you are having a bad hair day.—False alarm

Anytime you might be in danger of being physically hurt, your body's alarm bells should ring. This is how you know to keep yourself safe! It's important to listen to those alarm bells. But if you realize one of your anxiety alarms is false, try facing your fears and taking the risk.

REFLECTION:

When was a time when you had a false anxiety alarm but you believed it was a real alarm?

_____

_____

What are some real anxiety alarm bells you sometimes ignore?

_____

_____

LISTEN TO YOUR "SHOULDER ANGEL"

When you were a little kid, you may have seen a cartoon character who had a devil on one shoulder and an angel on the other.

The devil tried to tell the character to make a bad choice. The angel on the other shoulder tried to tell the character to make a good choice.

The devil might say something like, "Go ahead! Steal that! No one will notice." The angel might say, "Leave it alone. Stealing is wrong."

Obviously, you don't have a real devil and angel sitting on your shoulders. But you do have one part of your brain that tries to talk you into making bad choices, and another part of your brain that tries to talk you into making good choices.

These two voices can go against each other when it comes to taking risks. On one hand, you might be thinking, "Who will know if I cheat?" or, "Copying someone else's answers isn't that bad." On the other hand, you might be thinking, "Cheating is wrong!" or, "Don't let your eyes wander!"

The little voice that tries to talk you into making good choices is your conscience. But it might be easier to listen to your conscience if you think of it as your "shoulder angel."

When you're tempted to make a bad choice, take a deep breath and say to yourself, "Listen to my shoulder angel!" It might prevent you from taking bad risks. It also might push you to take calculated risks if they are good for you!

Traps to Avoid

Sometimes it's tough to know what is actually risky. Maybe you just watched a movie about killer snakes. And then you find yourself on the lookout for snakes everywhere! Just learning about snakes made you imagine you're at a bigger risk of getting bitten than you really are.

Of course, it's better to be cautious than to not care. (You should be careful of venomous snakes.) But sometimes our imaginations get the best of us. So pay attention to what's causing your anxiety alarm bells!

Also, keep in mind that just because a certain risk doesn't turn out the way you hoped, it doesn't mean it was a bad choice. You may have gotten turned down when you asked someone to go to the dance. Or maybe you got hurt playing soccer. This doesn't mean that you shouldn't have taken those risks. It just means that they didn't go the way you hoped this time.

QUICK TIPS

Learning how to calculate risks can help you make the best decisions for yourself. And that will help you become stronger and better! When you're struggling to take good risks, remind yourself of these exercises that will help you think big, feel good, and act brave.

THINK BIG: When you feel afraid, your brain will remind you of all the things that could go wrong. Argue the opposite so you can find the truth!

Feel GOOD: When something feels scary, figure out

whether you are having a real anxiety alarm or a false alarm. If it's a real alarm, take a step back. If it's a false alarm, keep going.

ACT BRAVE: When you are tempted to do something that you know is bad for you, listen to your shoulder angel!

7

They Create Their Future

Lucy couldn't remember much about what life was like when she still lived with both of her parents. But she was sure it was better than life right now!

She rarely saw her dad because he lived too far away. But sometimes she dreamed about what life would be like if she could live with him.

Her mother had remarried a long time ago, and Lucy wasn't exactly a fan of her new stepfather. Almost every sentence that came out of his mouth started with "People like us . . ."

What did that even mean?

When Lucy asked if she could get new sneakers, he laughed and said, "People like us can't afford expensive sneakers!" When the teacher recommended Lucy for the advanced math class, her stepdad said, "Those classes are for the super-smart kids, Lucy, not people like us."

One day, Lucy asked her mom, "When do you think I can get a phone?"

Her stepfather immediately chimed in and said, "People like us don't get their kids expensive smart-phones, Lucy. Don't get any big ideas!"

Lucy spun around and said, "I was talking to my mother, you know!"

Her stepfather yelled, "Don't you dare talk back to me, Lucy! I'm tired of you being so disrespectful. And I'm sick of your mother letting you act like a brat! That's why I have to speak up. She won't!"

Lucy ran to her room, buried her face in her pillow, and cried. Her stepfather was always such a jerk! Why did her mother let him treat her like that? What was wrong with them?

But then she started thinking, "Wait . . . what is wrong with us? What if I am like *them*?" Her stepfather's words, "people like us," kept playing in her head. Maybe *she* was one of *them*.

She started to think. "I'm not like the other kids at school. They have nice parents, they live in better places, and they are always doing fun things. They don't have to deal with the stuff I have to."

For a minute, she tried to imagine her adult life. She pictured herself living in an apartment just like the one she lived in now. She saw herself married to a jerk like her stepfather. And she imagined having kids who felt just like she did right now. Why? Because that's how "people like us" live!

She buried her face in the pillow a little deeper. She wished her parents had never split up or that she could live with her dad. Better yet, she even wished she could have been born into a totally different family!

Check Yourself

It's not helpful to worry *too much* about the future. But it's also a big mistake not to worry about the future at all! If you never make goals for yourself, you won't make good things happen. Check out these sentences below. See how many of them sound like you:

- ☐ I don't think much about what I want to be when I grow up.
- ☐ I can't really imagine what my life will be like in the future.
- ☐ I never set goals.
- ☐ I think my future is more determined by luck than hard work.
- ☐ I don't really plan ahead for anything.

☐ I don't even like to make plans with friends too far into the future.

☐ I don't think I have control over my adult life. Whatever happens, happens!

How much do these statements sound like you? If they sound a lot like you, you might be a little too relaxed about your future. Of course, it's important to enjoy being young. But you can't create a bright future without doing a little dreaming and planning along the way.

In this chapter, we'll talk about how to create a better future for yourself, why it's important, and how some exercises can help make it happen.

But first, let's get back to Lucy and her stepdad. . . .

 ## Closer Look

Lucy sat in social studies class waiting to see what she got on her latest project. It was a tough assignment that had involved a bunch of research on Latin American countries and then she had had to write a long report. She just hoped she did okay. But when she got her project back, she saw a lot of red ink on the page from her teacher.

Lucy's grade was horrible. She did the assignment completely wrong.

Her teacher had written across the top of the paper in red: "See me." So Lucy stayed after class. Her teacher said, "Lucy, I'm going to give you another chance to do this project. Read the instructions again and look at the notes I put on your report. Then give it another try."

Lucy was confused. She had worked so hard on this project! The idea of doing it all over again was the worst.

Plus, when she thought about doing the project all over again, her stepfather's voice kept repeating in her head, "People like us don't get good grades."

She thought, "I guess he's right! I *am* just like him! I even think like him now."

She figured there was no use in redoing her project. She would probably just get a bad grade again, anyway.

Hopefully, you don't have a parent or stepparent like Lucy's. Being raised by someone who thinks you can't succeed is tough. But if you do have someone like that in your life, you don't have to let their negativity drag you down.

Everyone can probably relate to Lucy on some level. We have all had times when we felt discouraged about our ability to live our dreams.

Maybe you've had times when you didn't even dare dream about your future. Perhaps you felt too hopeless (or silly) about thinking so big. This type of thinking will prevent you from creating your future.

There are many situations, people, and attitudes that might prevent you from making your life as good as it can be. Here are a few examples of things you might let stand in your way:

- **You let other people define you.** It doesn't matter if someone says you're not smart. And it doesn't matter if they call you a nerd. You have the power to be who you want to be (like we talked about in Chapter 2).

- **You don't ever set goals for yourself.** You might miss out on new opportunities if you don't create goals.

- **You don't challenge yourself.** Challenges can teach you a lot about yourself. They can teach you that you're more capable than you think!

- **You don't explore enough.** Explore a new museum! Explore the woods in your backyard! Curiosity and exploration can spark ideas about what kind of future you want for yourself.

- **You don't try hard enough.** You must put in effort to find out what you are capable of achieving.

REFLECTION:

What are some things you let stand in the way of creating a positive future for yourself?

_____

_____

PROOF POSITIVE

Lucy's teacher stopped her one day after class. She said, "Lucy! I'm surprised I haven't seen your project yet. What's going on?"

Lucy shrugged and said, "I'm not going to bother to redo it."

Her teacher looked shocked. "Why on earth would you choose that, Lucy? I know you can do a good job! A good grade on this project will help you get a much better grade in this class."

Lucy said, "I don't know why it matters if I get a better grade in this class. It's not like I'm going to use any of this later in life."

Her teacher said, "You never know, Lucy. You may want to visit other parts of the world when you're older. Tell you what. Tonight I want you to make a list of the top ten jobs you want to do when you're an adult. Bring it to me tomorrow. We'll talk about why you may need to know about other countries to do those jobs."

That night Lucy sat down and thought about the jobs she might want to do someday. She thought this would be a quick assignment, but she had never really thought about a career before. It took two hours to come up with a list.

When she returned to school the next day, she showed the list to her teacher. It included a bunch of careers, but her two favorites were scientist and marine biologist. Lucy's teacher sat down with her to read it. Together, they went through the whole list and discussed why knowing about foreign countries could be important in each profession.

Lucy loved the whole discussion. When they were done, her teacher said, "Lucy, this is a great list. And I know you can do any of these things if you put your mind to it."

Lucy beamed with pride!

For the first time ever, Lucy felt like she could create a happy future for herself. For a minute, she stopped thinking about everything her stepfather always said about "people like us." Now she began to think, "I'm someone who can . . ."

"Do I want to be a famous singer who lives in New York City? Do I want to start my own restaurant and live in a house near the beach?" She began to imagine endless possibilities.

Maybe, like Lucy, you've never really thought about what kind of life you want to live. Maybe you don't even know what you're going to do next week or next month, let alone next year!

Don't worry! You don't have to plan your whole life right now. Even most adults don't think that far ahead. But a little advance planning could help you create the best future possible. If you just sit around and wait to see what happens, then you will be stuck with just that . . . whatever happens.

Here are two examples of how creating your future can make you happier:

EXAMPLE 1—Wyatt waits to see what happens in life. Wyatt never thinks about what he wants to do after high school. Once he graduates, he doesn't do anything for a while. But then a family friend suggests he work for her at her store. Wyatt agrees. He works at the store part-time and continues living with his parents. He feels bored most of the time because his friends are busy with their own jobs or college. He doesn't earn much money, so he can't afford to do much anyway. So he spends a lot of time sitting at home and watching TV without any real plans for whatever comes next.

EXAMPLE 2—Wyatt creates a positive future.

Wyatt spends a lot of time trying new things. He discovers he loves to bake, and decides he wants to open his own bakery someday. When he's in high school, he learns as much as he can about baking and owning a business. When he graduates, he enrolls in a culinary arts program. This is when he makes plans to open his first bakery. He feels excited about life! He can't believe he will get paid to do something he loves every day!

Clearly, our second Wyatt enjoys life much more! Why? Because he designed the kind of life he wants to live by having big dreams and planning ahead.

Of course, creating your future isn't just about picking a career. You also will need to decide where you're going to live, who you're going to live with, and how you'll spend your time. Planning ahead will help you keep the most—and the best—options open.

REFLECTION:

What kind of life do you want to live?

_____

_____

HOW DID LUCY GROW STRONGER?

Lucy's outlook changed after talking to her teacher. She began thinking differently about herself and her ability.

From that day on, whenever her stepfather said things like, "People like us don't get to do those things," she gave herself a silent pep talk:

"People like *him* don't get to do those things. *I* can do those things someday if I want!"

Changing the way she thought about the future changed everything for her. She started trying new things and learning about more places. The more stuff she did, the more she kept thinking about the type of future she wanted. And her ideas kept getting bigger and bigger!

She knew she might not always get everything she wanted (she had to admit that becoming an astronaut, a

Broadway star, and a surgeon all at the same time might not be possible). But she also found out that she had the power to create a great life for herself. That made her feel good, and the better she felt, the easier it was to do brave things.

Exercises

THINK BIG

TALK TO YOURSELF LIKE A GOOD FRIEND

In the past, Lucy's brain had just replayed her stepfather's words on a loop. His words had always made her feel bad about herself. But once she started telling herself she could create her own future, her confidence improved, and she started to take more calculated risks (like we talked about in Chapter 6).

Like Lucy, you can also change the way you talk to yourself. Speaking to yourself with kindness can help you feel strong. But sometimes we speak to ourselves in some pretty mean ways—ways we would never talk to anyone else.

What if your friend said, "I am the dumbest person on the planet"? What would you say to that friend?

You probably wouldn't say, "Yep! You are an idiot!" You would say something kinder.

You might say, "Everyone fails tests sometimes. You're not dumb." Or maybe you'd say, "Stop it! You're really smart. You just made a mistake."

You probably don't speak to yourself so gently,

though. You might call yourself names. You might tell yourself you'll never succeed. And you might remind yourself of all the mistakes you've ever made. These types of conversations with yourself can keep you from building a bright future.

So start talking to yourself the same way you would talk to someone else. Ask yourself, "What would I say to a friend who had this idea?" or, "How would I respond to someone else who had this problem?" Then give yourself the same response.

Here are some examples:

- **What you might say to yourself:** "Everyone is going to laugh at me."
- **What you would say to a friend:** "You'll do great!"

- **What you might say to yourself:** "I'm so dumb."
- **What you would say to a friend:** "It was a hard test! Don't beat yourself up about it."

- **What you might say to yourself:** "I can't ever do anything right."
- **What you would say to a friend:** "You do lots of things really well!"

- What you might say to yourself: "I'll never get picked."
- What you would say to a friend: "You never know until you try!"

You can't create a great future if you're always putting yourself down. You probably wouldn't stay friends with someone if they always did that to you. So don't talk to yourself like that either! Practice cheering yourself on so you can stay motivated to create the best future for yourself.

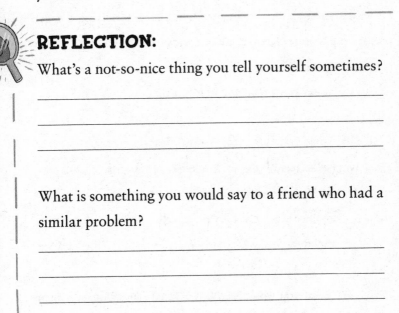

REFLECTION:

What's a not-so-nice thing you tell yourself sometimes?

_____

_____

_____

What is something you would say to a friend who had a similar problem?

_____

_____

_____

Feel GOOD

CREATE AN "IF . . . THEN" PLAN

When Lucy was tempted to avoid her assignment, she could have created an "if . . . then" plan. For example, when she thought there was no sense in doing her assignment, she could have told herself, "If I fail, then I'll ask my teacher for help." That could have given her more confidence. Sometimes we put things off because we're afraid something bad will happen. Or we don't do things because we doubt our ability. Creating a plan can help you feel better about moving forward!

Here are some examples of how you might create an "if . . . then" plan that builds you up:

SITUATION: You want to try out for the soccer team.

> **Worry:** "I might not make the team."
>
> **If . . . Then Plan:** "If I don't make the team, then I'll try another sport. Or I'll find something else fun to do with my time."

SITUATION: You get asked to present your science fair project in front of the whole school.

> **Worry:** "I might get so nervous that I forget what I'm going to say."

If . . . Then Plan: "If I get nervous, then I will take a deep breath and look at my notes."

SITUATION: You want to invite a friend to the movies with you.

Worry: "She might not want to hang out with me."

If . . . Then Plan: "If my friend says no, then I'll ask someone else to go with me."

When you have a good "if . . . then" plan in place, you'll feel better. And when you feel better, it becomes much easier to act brave.

REFLECTION:

Take a minute. Think about something you can do to create a better future for yourself. Now think of your biggest worry about doing it. Finally, create your own "if . . . then" plan.

If _____ happens . . .

(something negative)

then I will _____ .

(a positive way to respond)

ACT BRAVE

FIND YOUR PEOPLE

As long as Lucy was surrounded by people like her stepfather, she was going to struggle to succeed. His negative attitude made it hard for her to think positive.

Her teacher's positive attitude, however, helped her see things from a different point of view. When she changed her thinking, she felt better . . . and that made it easier to take action.

It's tough to imagine a bright future if you are surrounded by negative people with no motivation to become their best. If you are around people like that, they can drag you down, too.

If you want to feel inspired about your future, then surround yourself with motivated people. You want to be around other people who are doing amazing things. It can open your eyes to new possibilities. They might even challenge you to do new things too!

Of course, you might not have a very inspiring or supportive family. And maybe your friends aren't motivated like you are, either.

That's okay! You can still love them. But you can find some uplifting new people on your own, too. For example, you might join a club or activity with some kids who think more like you do.

Also, you can learn a lot from people you've never even met. Is there a famous person from history that you admire? Read books and articles about that person to find out what made them strong.

Maybe there's someone else in your life you want to learn more from—a teacher, a coach, or even a friend's parent. You might ask them some questions about how they decided to get into their careers. Ask them what their secret to being so happy is. Most adults are eager to share their experiences if a younger person asks them.

It takes courage to reach out and find your people. But doing so can change your life!

REFLECTION:

Who inspires you to become your best?

_____

_____

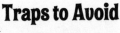

Traps to Avoid

Creating your future is not the same as wishful thinking. Sure, daydreaming is a lot of fun. It can help you imagine tons of different possibilities. But you don't get to where you want by just thinking about it. You have to take steps to get there.

Of course, your ideas about the future are probably going to change over time. This is normal! You may want to be a pro athlete at one point in your life. Then you might change your mind and want to be a doctor. It's okay to shift your dreams! The point is to have goals and to work hard to achieve them. As you grow and learn, your dreams will grow along with you.

There may also be times when you think other people are going to prevent you from creating the life you want. A teacher may give you a bad grade. A coach may cut you from the team. Just remember not to give them power over your future (like we talked about in Chapter 2). Sometimes these can be blessings in disguise that remind you to work harder.

QUICK TIPS

Strong kids create their futures. And while it can feel like hard work sometimes to create a positive future, it's well worth the effort. If you're struggling to make your future as good as it can be, remember these exercises that will help you think big, feel good, and act brave.

THINK BIG: Speak to yourself with the same kind words that you would say to a friend!

Feel GOOD: If you are hesitant about doing something, then create an "if . . . then" plan so you will know what to do if things go wrong. Having a plan can help you feel more confident.

ACT BRAVE: Surround yourself with inspiring people. Find people who want to create their own future . . . just like you!

8

They Own Their Mistakes

Parker stared inside his locker. Did he want to bring his math book home? If he did, his mother would know he had math homework. If he didn't bring it home, he could just tell her that his teacher gave the class the night off.

He thought for a minute. "I'll leave it here!" he decided.

When he got home, his mother asked what he had for homework. "Just a little Spanish," he said. He grabbed an apple and some chocolate milk. He sat down at the kitchen table and got to work. It took him about ten minutes to finish his Spanish paper. His mother commended him for being such a good worker. She even let him spend the rest of the night playing video games.

The next day he walked into math class with his unfinished homework.

He always hated math class. But today he really hated it!

He hated the look his teacher gave him when she saw he had slacked off again. He hated how she made impossible math problems look easy when she wrote them on the board. And he hated it when all the other kids understood, and he didn't.

At the end of class, his teacher assigned another worksheet. On top of that, she reminded everyone they had a test on Friday. Ugh. Parker hated math tests the most!

After class, he put his math book back in his locker. This time, he covered it with his hoodie. He didn't even want to *look* at his math book.

For the rest of the week, the only time he touched his math book was when he brought it to class. He never put it in his backpack, and he never brought it home.

Basically, he pretended math didn't exist! Avoiding math as much as possible helped him feel better—at least for a little bit.

But once math test day rolled around, there was no more avoiding it. He sat at his desk and stared at his test. He had no idea how to answer any of the questions.

When time was up, his teacher collected the papers. All he had written on his page was his name. His teacher looked confused and said, "You didn't take your test?"

Parker looked up at his teacher and told her the truth. "I did all of it that I could."

He knew he had messed up. And he hadn't just messed up the test—he had messed up by not doing his homework and not asking for help before it was too late.

Check Yourself

Everyone makes mistakes sometimes. That's okay! What really matters is how you respond to your mistakes. Do you own them? Or do you hide them? Check out the sentences below. See how many of them sound like you:

- [ ] When I mess up, I don't try to figure out what went wrong.
- [ ] I sometimes say, "I won't do that again." But then I do it again!
- [ ] I give up after I make a mistake.
- [ ] People accuse me of making excuses for my mistakes.
- [ ] I try to hide my mistakes. I don't want anyone to know I messed up!
- [ ] I think mistakes are proof I'm not good enough.
- [ ] If I can't do something perfectly the first time, I would rather not try.

How much do these sentences sound like you? The more those ring true, the less likely you are to own your mistakes. That means you might be doomed to repeat the same mistakes over and over again, and you are probably making life harder for yourself. But the good news is you can learn to turn your mistakes into life lessons. Coming up, we'll find out how to recognize your mistakes, how to own them, and how to keep from repeating them!

But first, let's get back to Parker and his math. . . .

Closer Look

Parker felt dumb that he didn't understand his math assignments. He thought he was the only one struggling in the class.

So it felt better for him to ignore his problem—at least at first. When he didn't bring his math book home, he could avoid doing his homework. At least when he wasn't thinking about math, he didn't feel stupid.

So he spent his evenings playing video games instead. He felt relaxed and happy. He figured he deserved to, since school was so stressful. He didn't need to stress about schoolwork at night too!

But the longer he avoided his work, the farther behind he fell, and the bigger his problems grew.

Perhaps you can relate to Parker. Owning your mistakes and taking responsibility for them can be a tough thing to do.

Sometimes mistakes come from *not* doing something (like *not* having a difficult conversation or *not* asking for help).

Other times, mistakes come from doing something you shouldn't do (like yelling at your mom or posting something mean on social media).

Here are some situations to show the difference between owning your mistake and hiding your mistake:

SITUATION: You got in trouble at school. You were sent to the principal's office!

- **Owning your mistake:** You tell your parents about it when you get home.
- **Hiding your mistake:** You hope they don't find out.

SITUATION: You shared some juicy gossip about a friend. Now your friend hears you've been spreading the rumor.

- **Owning your mistake:** You admit that you spread the rumor and apologize.
- **Hiding your mistake:** You lie and say you never said it.

SITUATION: You spill soda all over the living room carpet. When you try to clean it up, the stain spreads.

- **Owning your mistake:** You go tell your parents what happened.
- **Hiding your mistake:** You look for something to put over that part of the carpet so they won't notice the stain.

Sometimes it takes more effort to hide a mistake than it does to just own it. And if you waste all your energy hiding a mistake, you might be more likely to repeat it instead of learning from it.

If you're not careful, you might repeat mistakes more than once.

REFLECTION:

What's an example of a time when you hid your mistake?

_____

_____

_____

What made it hard to own your mistake?

_____

_____

_____

PROOF POSITIVE

Parker felt terrible when he got a zero on his math test. He knew his mother was going to be upset. That day he didn't eat much at lunch. When a friend asked him what was wrong, Parker told her what happened.

His friend said, "Oh no! What if you get held back?"

Parker hadn't even thought about that! Now he had even more reason to worry.

The huge problems he now faced all started with one small mistake that he kept repeating. It was sort of like a chain reaction.

Here's how one mistake led to another . . . and another:

1. He didn't ask the teacher for help understanding the assignment.
2. He stopped bringing his math book home.
3. He lied to his mom and said he didn't have math homework.
4. He didn't do his assignments.

Those mistakes caused him to get zeros on homework assignments, and he fell farther behind. Then he didn't understand a single question on the test . . . and got another zero.

Each time he made a mistake, he had an opportunity

to make things better. But instead of facing his mistakes head on, he pretended they didn't happen. It was like he was digging himself into a hole that just kept getting deeper and deeper. Soon he felt like there was no way to dig himself out!

Like Parker, you may have had times when learning from one mistake could have saved you a lot of hassle down the road. But you didn't grow from that first mistake. You didn't own it!

It's tough to own mistakes. It's hard to say, "Hey, I messed up." It's even tempting to lie or cover things up to try to make problems go away. But when we do those things, it means we aren't learning from our mistakes. And most of the time that leads to even bigger problems.

Here's why it's helpful to own your mistakes and learn from them the first time you make them:

- **You increase your chances of reaching your goals.**
  You might have goals to improve your grades or to eat healthier. If you learn from each mistake, you can do better next time.
- **You'll think more positively about yourself.**
  When you keep making mistakes, you might think that you're not good enough. But if you learn from those mistakes,

you'll prove to yourself that you can do better!

- **You'll solve problems.**

  When you avoid problems, you get stuck making the same mistakes. Solving each problem will help you get ahead.

- **You'll try harder.**

  When you figure out what you did wrong, you also discover how to do it better. Now you are ready to try harder next time.

REFLECTION:

What's an example of a time when you owned your mistake?

_____

_____

HOW DID PARKER GROW STRONGER?

Right after Parker got a zero on his test, the teacher emailed his mother. She told her that Parker was also missing several homework assignments.

When Parker got home that afternoon, his mother said, "We need to talk about math." Math was the last thing Parker wanted to talk about. But his mother insisted he sit down at the table so they could discuss what was going on.

Parker said, "I don't know what's going on! I mean . . . nothing is going on. You don't have to make it a big deal!"

He hoped if he got frustrated enough, his mother would just leave him alone. Of course, she didn't leave him alone, though. She insisted they address this issue right here, right now.

So they had a long talk. Parker explained that he didn't understand his math assignments. And once he fell behind, he didn't know how to get caught back up.

When he was done talking, she said, "First things first. You're grounded for lying to me. You said you didn't have any math homework when you did. But we also have to fix this situation so that it doesn't happen again."

She and Parker created a plan together that would help dig him out of the deep hole he had dug. The new plan was this: Parker would ask his teacher for help tomorrow. He would do extra homework every night to get caught up. And his mother would check up on him every day to make sure he was staying on top of his work.

When he got caught up on his work, he would no longer be grounded.

Parker felt bad that he had lied to his mother. He was embarrassed about the zeros he had gotten. And he was frustrated that he was grounded.

But now he also felt a little relieved that this was going to be over soon. And he felt hopeful that their new plan could help him get unstuck.

Exercises

THINK BIG

REPLACE PROBLEM THOUGHTS WITH SOLUTION THOUGHTS

Whenever Parker thought about math, he thought about not knowing the answers. He was only thinking about the problem. He never looked for solutions!

When you make a mistake, you might be tempted to do the same thing—focus on everything you did wrong. You probably think a lot about how you messed up. You might wonder how you could have been so dumb. And you may worry that someone else noticed you failed.

But these types of thoughts are not helpful. They can easily drag you down and make you feel even worse. If you feel worse, you might not try again!

Here's an example of one of Parker's problem thoughts:

- **Parker's problem thought:** "I'm so stupid! I can't figure out any of my math."

    Parker's problem thoughts caused him to feel worse. And they made him avoid trying to fix the problem.

    If he had developed a solution thought, he may

have felt better. And he may have come up with a solution like this:

- **Parker's solution thought:** "I don't understand how to do this. I will ask my teacher to help me!"

   Focusing on the solution, instead of the problem, could have kept Parker from making more mistakes.

Here are some more ways you might respond to a problem thought with a solution thought:

- **Problem thought:** "I can't believe I missed the ball!"
- **Solution thought:** "I'll keep my eye on the ball better next time."

- **Problem thought:** "I can't control my temper! I always say things that hurt people's feelings."
- **Solution thought:** "Next time I get upset, I'll calm down before I say anything."

- **Problem thought:** "I'm so awkward! I never say anything when I'm around other kids."
- **Solution thought:** "I'll relax and talk a little more tomorrow at recess."

When you make a mistake, don't dwell on everything you did wrong. Beating yourself up for a mistake won't motivate you to do better next time.

Remember when we talked about BLUE thoughts in Chapter 1? Problem thoughts are often BLUE thoughts. The next time you need to come up with a solution thought, you might try turning your BLUE thoughts into true thoughts first.

This can also be a good time to use the STEPS to problem-solving like we talked about in Chapter 3. Going through the STEPS can help you create a solution thought as well.

REFLECTION:

Think about a time when you had a problem thought. Now take a minute to think about a solution thought you could have developed.

_____

_____

Feel GOOD

CREATE A CALM-DOWN KIT

Parker didn't know how to take care of his feelings in a healthy way. So he did things that made him feel good in the moment.

But he only created bigger problems for himself in the future by doing this. He played video games instead of doing his homework. This made him happy for a little while. But it made things worse later.

He traded feeling a little bad now for feeling really bad later. He may have felt a little frustrated when he tried to do his homework. But he felt much worse when he got zeros on his assignments, lied to his mother, and bombed the test.

PARKER'S PROBLEM:

He felt anxious about not knowing how to do his math homework.

A SOLUTION THAT COULD HAVE HELPED PARKER:

Parker could have created a calm-down kit to deal with his feelings. Then he could have done his homework and avoided the bigger problems that came later.

Mistakes can cause you to feel a lot of uncomfortable emotions. You may feel embarrassed when you mess up. After all, what will other people think?

You might be mad at yourself for not doing as well as you had hoped. And you may be a little jealous of other people who succeeded when you didn't. It's okay.

Feelings like this will happen. Just don't let those feelings keep you stuck.

Remember in Chapter 1 when we talked about how to figure out if your feelings were a friend or an enemy? (And if they are an enemy, you can use a mood booster to cheer yourself up.) Well, when your unhelpful feelings include anger or anxiety, a calm-down kit may be in order.

Here's why: it's tough to avoid a mistake when you're feeling anxious. And it's impossible to learn from your mistake if you feel so angry your head might explode! You need to calm your emotions first. Then you can work on the solution.

Create a calm-down kit to help you feel good again. Fill an old shoebox with activities that will calm your mind and your body. It's *your* box—so the items in it should be things that you pick.

Here are some examples of what someone might include in their box:

- A playlist of songs that calm you down
- Scented candles or incense
- A worry stone
- A stress ball
- Pictures of your family, friends, or pets
- A joke book

- Paper and colored pencils
- A puzzle
- Your favorite candy

Try to include activities in your box that you can *do*. Things you can touch, hear, smell, and taste. Keep your calm-down kit in a place that's easy to get to, like in your closet or on your bookshelf.

When you make a mistake and you're feeling upset, go get your calm-down kit!

Similar to the way mood boosters raise feelings of happiness (like we talked about in Chapter 1), calm-down kits lower your anger, frustration, and anxiety. When you're feeling calmer, you can own your mistakes and learn from them, instead of avoiding and repeating them.

REFLECTION:

What can you put in your own calm-down kit?

_____

_____

What are some times when you may want to use your calm-down kit?

_____

_____

ACT BRAVE

SET YOURSELF UP FOR SUCCESS

Sometimes we make one mistake and we want to give up. We decide "It just wasn't meant to be" or, "I'm just not someone who is ever going to be good at that." So we set ourselves up for failure before we really begin to try.

That's what Parker did.

- **Parker set himself up for failure:**
  He didn't ask for help. He didn't bring his math book home. And he didn't do his assignments. No wonder he failed his test!

- **Parker could have set himself up for success:**
  He could have asked his teacher for help. He could have told his mother he needed help. And he could also have set aside time every day to work on math. He would have done much better on the test!

Setting yourself up for success means doing something that makes it easier for you to do better next time.

Here are some examples of how you might do that:

- **Mistake:** You forget to bring your sneakers to school on gym day.

- **Setup for success:** Set an alert on your phone that reminds you to pack your sneakers the night before.

- **Mistake:** You spend all your allowance money every time you go to the store. You can never save up for that thing you really want to buy.
- **Setup for success:** You bring just a little bit of money with you to the store, so you can't spend it all.

- **Mistake:** You play video games and lose track of time. You forget to do your chores and get in trouble.
- **Setup for success:** Do your chores first. Then play video games without worrying!

When you make a mistake, create your solution thought and use your calm-down kit if you need it. Then set yourself up for success so you don't repeat the mistake again.

REFLECTION:

What's an example of a mistake that you often make?

_____

_____

_____

Traps to Avoid

There's an old saying "get back on the horse." In other words, if you fall off a horse, you should get right back on and keep on going. There's some truth to this. You don't want to waste too much time thinking about what went wrong. Sometimes you just have to jump right back into action so you don't overthink the problem.

But jumping into action too quickly can cause problems, too. You might not learn anything if you just keep taking action. Sometimes you need to pause for a minute to think about how you'll do things differently next time.

Another problem to think about is that you won't always be able to reach for your calm-down kit when you need it. Let's say you miss a foul shot during a basketball game. You have to take the second shot right away. In times like these, your only option is to talk to yourself in a helpful way.

If you catch yourself thinking something like, "Oh

great, you just blew it, stupid!" then remind yourself, "That's okay. I have another chance. I'll make this one!" That's when talking to yourself like a friend comes in handy (like we discussed in Chapter 6).

QUICK TIPS

Strong kids own their mistakes and then learn from them. Of course, that's tough to do sometimes. But learning from mistakes helps you grow stronger and become better. So the next time you're struggling to learn from your mistakes, practice these exercises that will help you think big, feel good, and act brave.

THINK BIG: Replace your problem thoughts with solution thoughts.

Feel GOOD: Create a calm-down kit. Use it when you are feeling angry or frustrated. When you're feeling calmer, you can make better decisions.

ACT BRAVE: Make it easier to avoid repeating your mistakes by setting yourself up for success!

9

They Celebrate Other People's Success

When Olivia sat down for lunch, Emma said, "Guess what? My parents are going to let me have Snapchat!" Olivia forced a smile and said, "Oh, that's cool."

But Olivia didn't really think it was cool. She was jealous. It was just one more thing Emma had that she didn't. Olivia's parents weren't going to let her use Snapchat anytime soon.

Emma got good grades, wore brand-name clothes, and all the cute boys liked her. And Emma wasn't the only one.

Camila was practically a rock star, too! She was pretty, she was a volleyball star, and her family was so rich that they had a second house.

Olivia liked Emma and Camila—they were all BFFs. But she felt she could never keep up with them.

These days, Camila couldn't stop talking about how excited she was for her birthday party. It was going to be a pool party. Then they were going to watch an outdoor movie in Camila's backyard. And the night was going to end with a bonfire!

As soon as Camila arrived at the lunch table, she announced the latest birthday update—like she always did. "Austin said he's coming to my party!" she said. Olivia stayed quiet and took a bite of her sandwich. Then Camila added, "Oh! And did I tell you my parents said we could get a DJ? We were just going to have my cousin play music, but we decided to hire a professional DJ instead!"

"We know! You told us at least ten times, Camila!" Olivia said.

Camila frowned. She replied, "Well, you don't have to be rude about it, Olivia."

No one said a word for a minute. Emma broke the awkward silence by telling a random story about something that happened in gym. Olivia stayed quiet for the rest of lunch.

That night Olivia texted Emma, saying, "Camila is so annoying. All she can talk about is her stupid party!"

Emma replied, "She's just excited, Olivia. You don't have to be so weird about it!"

And with that text, Olivia felt more alone than ever.

Check Yourself

It can be hard to be happy for other people sometimes. It can be especially hard to celebrate other people's success if it involves something you wanted for yourself. Check out the following sentences and see how many of them sound like you.

- ☐ I'm jealous when my friends get stuff I want.
- ☐ I hate it when my classmates get better grades than I do.
- ☐ I don't like it when my friends beat me in sports!
- ☐ I compare how I look with everyone else.
- ☐ It's hard to feel happy for my friends when they succeed.
- ☐ Sometimes I brag about myself to feel better.
- ☐ When something bad happens to one of my friends, I secretly feel a little bit happy.

Do many of those sound familiar? If so, you might have trouble celebrating other people's success. Know that you're not alone though. Many people struggle with this problem, but there are steps you can take to deal with it. In this chapter, we'll talk about why it's important to celebrate other people's success, and the exercises that can help you do that.

But first, let's get back to Olivia and her friends. . . .

 ## Closer Look

Olivia's friends liked to talk about the good things in their lives. And when they did, it made her think about all the good things that *weren't* happening in her life.

She could just imagine what Camila's party was going to be like. Tons of people would be giving Camila attention and congratulating her for throwing such a great party. After that, everyone in school would start liking Camila even more than they did now!

Olivia remembered her own birthday party. She had five friends come over to her house and they ate a cake her mother made. She sure didn't have a pool, a DJ, or a bonfire!

Why couldn't she have a party like Camila? And why couldn't she have Snapchat like Emma?

On top of that, why did Emma have to take sides with Camila? No one understood her pain! At least that's what Olivia thought.

Maybe you can relate to the things Olivia was feeling. Maybe you have felt jealous or left out before, too. That can make it hard to celebrate when someone else wins.

Someone else's strengths might also cause you to think about your weaknesses. If your friend earns the Most Valuable Player award in soccer, you might start to imagine you're a bad player. As you watch them accept their award, you might think, "I'll never be that good. I should just quit now!"

Maybe you feel the same way when your friend gets a better grade than yours, or when your sibling earns a reward you didn't get.

Sometimes we get a little upset if we think people are doing better than we are. This might cause us to deal with our hurt feelings in unhelpful ways. Instead of cheering someone on or celebrating with them, we might be tempted to do hurtful things.

Here are the four types of roles you might play when you hear someone else's good news:

1. The Downplayer

SITUATION: Your mother says your little brother is a star on the soccer field.

You act like what they did was no big deal. You say, "Well, it's easy to be the star of the team when no one else is any good!"

2. The Pretender

SITUATION: Your friend gets a better grade on a test than you.

You pretend you didn't want it anyway. You shrug and say, "I didn't even study. I don't care about grades!"

3. The Bragger

SITUATION: Your friend announces that his family is going on an amazing vacation over spring break.

You brag about yourself. You say, "I'm doing something even better than that! I just can't say it yet 'cause it's a secret."

4. The Attention Seeker

SITUATION: Your friend announces that her family is going to get a puppy.

You turn it around and make it about you. You say, "Lucky you. That's so not fair! My parents will never let me get a dog."

Have you ever played any of those parts? A lot of us have at one time or another.

Fortunately, you can choose to be "the supporter" if you put your mind to it. Up next, we'll talk about why you might want to cheer others on.

PROOF POSITIVE

When Olivia sent that text to Emma complaining about Camila, she expected Emma to agree with her. But instead, Emma called _her_ out for being rude!

Olivia couldn't believe Emma took Camila's side. It hurt her feelings. "Fine!" she thought. "If the two of them are going to gang up on me, I won't talk to either of them."

The next morning, she didn't say much to Camila or Emma at school. She nodded when they talked. But she stayed quiet.

She made sure to act extra friendly to other kids though. Olivia wanted Emma and Camila to see she wasn't in a bad mood. She was only mad at them.

Lunchtime rolled around. Olivia planned to keep giving them the cold shoulder. At some point, she knew they would realize that they were being jerks to her.

She walked toward their usual lunch table, and what did she see? Camila was crying, and Emma had her arm over her shoulder. Olivia thought, "Yep! I bet they finally realized they were shutting me out. They probably feel super bad about it!"

She got to the table and asked, "What's going on?" She waited for an apology.

Both girls stayed silent for a minute, until Emma looked up and said, "Camila's parents are getting divorced."

Olivia's heart dropped. She didn't even know how to respond. She had no idea Camila was going through something like this.

As she watched Camila crying, Olivia thought, "Wow! Maybe I'm the one who has been a jerk around here. Not them."

She sat down and asked her, "When did this happen, Camila?" Camila said her dad had moved out a few months ago. Apparently, Emma had known about it for a while.

At first Olivia was upset that Camila hadn't told

her. But then she thought about it. She had been so rude to Camila lately because of her own jealousy. She'd been ignoring a lot of Camila's texts and calls. And whenever Camila tried to talk about anything going on in her life, Olivia changed the subject because she thought anything Camila said about her home life would somehow turn into her talking about her party again. It's no wonder that Camila didn't feel comfortable telling her this secret. Olivia's feelings of jealousy were getting in the way of helping her friend.

Perhaps you can relate to some of the feelings Olivia had. Maybe you have felt jealous in the past, too. You may have thought you deserved some of the things your friends have. Or maybe you just didn't want them to win . . . at anything. Helping others will help you build important friendships. Here's how:

- **People like supportive people.** You can go out for ice cream to celebrate your sibling's most recent report card. You can attend your friend's dance recital and applaud her afterward. Whatever you do, support your people!

- **You can learn from them.** You can learn from people who are winning. Figure out what they are doing right, and those things might work for you, too!

- **They'll be more likely to celebrate with you, too.** When something is going well in your life, you are going to want people there to cheer you on. Those people will remember what you did for them and try to show up for you, too!

REFLECTION:

What's a time when you celebrated someone else's success?

_____

How did it feel?

_____

HOW DID OLIVIA GROW STRONGER?

Olivia managed to apologize to Camila. "I'm sorry that you are going through this, Camila! And I'm sorry I haven't been a good friend. I've been a little jealous over this party that you're throwing. I never imagined you were going through such tough times."

They spent the rest of lunch talking about the things Camila was dealing with. Her parents fought so much. And her mom and dad kept putting her in the middle of their arguments. It gave Camila stress almost all the time.

She said, "I think my parents are just throwing this party for me because they feel guilty. But it can never make up for what they put me through."

Listening to Camila made Olivia realize a few things:

- **She was comparing two completely different situations.** Her friends' lives weren't better or worse than hers. They were just different.

- **She didn't know the whole story.** Olivia realized that she had no idea what was really going on in her friends' lives. They were struggling with things she didn't know about.

- **She wasn't in competition.** She realized there is no prize for the person who has the best life. They were friends. And they all needed to support each other.

Realizing those things helped Olivia see everything in a new light. She wanted to work on becoming a better friend. She wanted to be the kind of friend who could cheer her pals on when they were winning in life. After all, if she didn't cheer for them, who would?

Exercises

THINK BIG

OPEN THE SHOEBOX

Olivia was comparing her inside to other people's outsides. She didn't realize one important thing. People who look like they have everything on the outside might not feel good on the inside. And you can't tell just by looking at someone.

A good way to picture it is to think of a shoebox. Imagine that you decorate the inside of the shoebox with words and pictures that describe how you feel. No one but you will ever see the inside of this box.

Now imagine that you're going to decorate the outside of the box for everyone to see. What would you want them to think about you?

Maybe the inside of the box would reveal your sadness or your fears. It might show that you worry about how you look. It might reveal that you sometimes wonder whether you're good enough.

But the outside of the box would probably only include the things you like. Maybe you would decorate it with drawings of your favorite emojis. You might have pictures of dogs, fast cars, or your favorite singers and athletes. You might even paint a picture of a beautiful beach or skyline.

You would want people to see the cool things about your personality, right? Well, so does everyone else! So you only see the outside of their boxes, too. They probably have many of the same doubts and fears that you have on the inside as well. They just hide them inside their box, like you probably do.

When you catch yourself thinking things like, "His life is better than mine," or, "People always like him more," remind yourself that you aren't in competition. Comparing your inside to someone else's outside makes no sense!

REFLECTION:

Take a minute and imagine what the inside of your shoebox would look like. Now imagine the outside of your shoebox. How are they different?

_____

_____

Would people be surprised to see the inside of your shoebox?

_____

_____

Feel GOOD

"WALK A MILE IN SOMEONE ELSE'S SHOES"

Olivia got so focused on how *she* was feeling that she lost sight of how her friends might be feeling. If she could have paused for a minute, she might have wondered why Camila was only talking about her party.

If she could have walked a mile in her friend's shoes, Olivia might have been able to act like a better friend. "Walking a mile in someone else's shoes" is an exercise that can remind you that other people have feelings, too. If you understand how someone else feels, you will be more understanding of them. And that may help you feel better about celebrating someone else's success.

Feeling a little bit of jealousy sometimes is normal. But you don't want to stay stuck in those jealous feelings. Walking a mile in someone else's shoes might help you feel better, so you can get unstuck!

When you notice you're struggling to cheer someone on, take a minute to name your feelings (like we talked about in Chapter 3). Are you sad? Jealous? Frustrated?

Then walk a mile in the other person's shoes. Imagine being that other person for a minute. Think about what they have going on in their lives.

Now take a minute to think about how that person is feeling. Are they happy? Excited? Sad? Nervous?

You might even make a face that shows how you think the other person is feeling. Experts have found that when you make a certain face, you actually feel that emotion! So if you smile when you imagine the other person feels happy, you'll feel happy for a second. And it'll remind you that the other person has emotions, too. That's easy to forget when you're feeling upset. But when you remind yourself of that, it becomes easier to cheer them on.

So next time you go to your brother's baseball game, cheer for him! If your friend wins the spelling bee, call her and tell her you are happy for her! Always look for ways to cheer others on.

REFLECTION:

Think of someone in your life who might benefit from you cheering them on right now. Take a minute to walk in their shoes.

How might that person be feeling right now?

_____

_____

How might they feel different if you cheer them on?

_____

_____

ACT BRAVE

ACT LIKE THE TYPE OF PERSON YOU WANT TO BE

Olivia wanted to be a good friend, but her constant comparison and envy got in the way. If only she had known she could *act* like a good friend even when she wasn't *feeling* it.

Sometimes, changing your behavior first can change the way you feel. In other words, act like the type of person you want to become, and the thoughts and feelings will follow.

This doesn't mean copying someone though. We are not talking about imitating an older teenager or a celebrity. Instead, it's about acting like the *type* of person you want to be.

Here are some examples:

- **If you want to be a confident person, then act confident.**
  Look people in the eye when you talk to them. Raise your hand and speak up!

- **If you want to be the kind of person who has a lot of friends, then act friendly.**
  Meet new people. Strike up cool conversations. Really listen to what others have to say.

- **If you want to be a good student, then act like a good student.**
  Study hard. Do your homework. Ask questions. And keep learning.

Acting like the person you want to become isn't acting fake or being someone you're not. It's about acting like the best version of yourself that you can be. Over time, you'll start to think and feel like that person, too!

When you focus on becoming the person you want to be, you won't worry so much about what other people are doing. It won't matter whether your friends have higher grades or whether they do better in sports. You will be so focused on becoming your best self that you won't care about trying to compete with them.

So if you are ever struggling to feel happy for someone else, act like a supporter anyway. You might find that cheering someone on helps you feel better!

REFLECTION:

What can you do to act like a supporter when someone in your life does something good?

_____

_____

Traps to Avoid

Sometimes we imagine that other people have better lives. But it's not always just in our heads. Some kids you meet will be more fortunate than you in some ways.

They may come from families with more money. Or they might always get higher grades than you. But even if those things are facts, you don't have to let their success cause you to feel bad.

Some people will have things that you don't—that is reality. But you'll also have some things that they won't have in life. And that's okay! Life is not about competing for the most stuff.

Social media can make it really tough to celebrate other people's success. Every time you scroll through social media, you might start to think that everyone else is happier and having more fun than you are.

210

But always remember that people are only sharing what they want you to see (like the outside of the shoebox we talked about earlier). They aren't sharing all the stuff they feel on the inside. Remind yourself of this when you are tempted to compare your real life to the life someone else posts on social media.

QUICK TIPS

Strong kids celebrate other people's success. But that can be tough to do sometimes. When you find it hard to be happy for other people, remember these exercises that can help you think big, feel good, and act brave.

THINK BIG: Think of the example of decorating the shoebox. Don't compare your inside to someone else's outside!

Feel GOOD: If you feel jealous, try to walk a mile in someone else's shoes. You might find that thinking about their feelings helps you understand them better and even feel happier for them.

ACT BRAVE: Act like the type of person you are trying to become. The thoughts and feelings will follow!

10

They Fail and Try Again

Max started playing basketball when he was four years old. It was one of his favorite things to do.

He was one of the shortest kids on the school team. But he was fast, and he could handle the ball better than most.

His team was good this year, too! He had been playing with some of his teammates for years. Now they knew each other well, and their comfort level with each other definitely helped them dominate on the court.

As the school's basketball season began to wind down, there was a lot of talk about a travel team. It was a special team that only took the best players from a bunch of different schools. Most of the boys in Max's group were planning to try out.

When Max showed up for one of his final school games of the year, his friends were in the locker room talking about the travel team again.

"Hey, Max! You're going to do the travel team, too, right?" one friend asked.

Max said, "For sure! I'm not ready for basketball to be over yet!"

Another boy said, "It sounds like most of us are trying out. I wonder how many of us will actually make it."

Max said, "I hope we *all* make it!"

His teammate said, "Well, at least you know you'll make the team, Max. You're good!"

Max smiled and shrugged. He said, "You never know." But deep down, he did know. He was pretty much the best player on his school team.

A few weeks later, Max went to the travel-team tryouts. Some of the guys from other schools were already playing on the court.

His teammates were waiting to warm up. One of them said, "These guys look pretty good!"

Max tried to make him feel better. "Don't psych yourself out already! Just go out there and show them what you can do." Then he added, "These other schools will see that we're really the best!"

With that, Max walked out to the court.

The coaches broke the boys up into different teams, and they began to play. The kid guarding Max was tall and fast! In fact, he was faster than anyone he had ever played against. Max struggled to even get the ball. He only took a few shots the whole game—and he scored way fewer points than usual. He felt pretty discouraged.

The next day, as planned, the coaches called the parents to announce who made the team. Max's dad got the call. That night, he sat Max down and said, "I have to tell you something." Max could tell from the look on his father's face that this wasn't good.

His father said, "I have good news and bad news. The good news is you can play basketball for the travel league! The bad news is you didn't make it on to their A-team. You made the B-team."

Max didn't know they had a B-team. He had no idea what that even meant. But he did know B didn't stand for "Best!" Max didn't want to be on any team that wasn't for the best kids. If he couldn't be on the A-team, he wasn't going to play!

Check Yourself

Failing feels awful! It can be frustrating, embarrassing, and depressing. If you're not careful, you might let failure keep you down and prevent you from trying again. Take a minute to read over the statements below. How many of these describe you?

- [ ] I only want to do things if I do them really well.
- [ ] If I'm not good at something, I usually give up right away.
- [ ] Rather than fail at something really big, I'd rather not try at all.
- [ ] I think failing is one of the worst things that could happen to anyone.
- [ ] Whenever I fail, I think I'm a loser.
- [ ] I try to make sure no one knows when I fail.
- [ ] I make excuses when I don't win or succeed.

Do any of these sound like you? The more they do, the more likely you are to give up after your first failure. You might even avoid trying something in the first place.

Failure can be a great learning experience though. And failing a few times could actually even help you succeed in the end. In this chapter, we'll talk about how to conquer the fear of failure, how it can help you succeed, and the best strategies for bouncing back.

But first, let's get back to Max and basketball. . . .

 ## Closer Look

When Max learned that he made the B-team, he went

to his room to be alone for a bit. Within a few minutes, he got a group text from his teammates. Two of them announced they'd made the A-team.

Max couldn't believe it! His dad seemed a little surprised, too. But he said, "That's okay, Max. Maybe they just did better at tryouts than you did."

These words stung Max so bad that he felt like he couldn't breathe for a minute. He couldn't speak. All he could think about was the fact that he never wanted to feel like this ever again. He would rather not play basketball than risk being rejected!

Maybe you've felt like Max before. Maybe you really wanted something, but you failed to make it happen. So you were faced with a tough choice: Do I give up? Or do I bounce back?

Here are some examples of how giving up is different than bouncing back:

SITUATION: You get a bad grade on a science project.

- **Giving up:** You decide that you are bad at science. You won't put any effort into science ever again!
- **Bouncing back:** You ask your teacher to help you figure out what you did wrong. You work on it. And you do better on your next assignment.

SITUATION: You invite someone to the dance. That person says no.

- **Giving up:** You don't go to the dance. You tell yourself it wasn't going to be fun, anyway.
- **Bouncing back:** You ask someone else to go to the dance with you.

SITUATION: You tell your neighbor you are available to babysit their kids. The neighbor hires someone else.

- **Giving up:** You stop talking to the neighbor. You give up on trying to get a job.
- **Bouncing back:** You tell other family friends and neighbors that you can do babysitting jobs.

Bouncing back is tough! You have to deal with uncomfortable feelings. You have to risk failing again. And you have to put in extra work to try to succeed the next time.

But sometimes trying again is worth the effort!

REFLECTION:

What's an example of a time that you failed and then gave up?

_____

_____

PROOF POSITIVE

Max stayed in his room for a while. He didn't reply to his teammates' messages because he wasn't ready to tell them he only made the B-team.

Max's dad knocked on his door. When Max let him in, his dad said, "I just wanted to let you know that your first practice is right after school tomorrow."

Max said, "Huh? Oh, no! I'm not going. I'm not going to be on the B-team!"

His dad said, "I know it's not what you wanted, Max. You don't have to like it. But you also don't have to act like a sore loser."

"Oh, that's nice, Dad! Real nice!" Max said as he fought back tears. "You're calling me a loser?"

His dad sighed. "That's not what I meant. I said you are *acting* like a sore loser because you didn't get a spot on the A-team. You can choose to have a better attitude about this." He finished by saying, "I expect you to go to practice tomorrow." Then he walked out.

Max was devastated. He couldn't believe his dad

expected him to stay on the B-team. His dad didn't understand that Max didn't *just* want to quit the B-team. He was never trying out for another team again!

Here's what Max was experiencing:

- **Max's thoughts:** "I guess I'm not such a good basketball player after all. If I was really good, then I would have made the A-team."
- **Max's feelings:** disappointment, embarrassment, sadness, frustration
- **Max's actions:** He planned to avoid any rejection in the future (whatever the cost).

Avoiding situations where he might get rejected would keep him from having bad feelings. But doing this also meant that he would have to give up a lot of things—including his favorite sport.

Have you ever not been picked for something? You might understand what Max was going through. When you fail, sometimes the last thing you want to do is try again. It's because failing feels bad! And most of us will do anything not to feel bad.

But here are some reasons why you might want to try again after you fail:

- **Failure can actually help you succeed.**

  If you had given up the first time you fell down as a baby, would you have ever learned to walk? Of course not! But every time you fell down, you learned a little more about how to get better at walking.

- **You can handle failure.**

  Your brain might try to tell you that you can't handle failure. But it's not the end of the world! It just feels bad for a little while.

- **Failure is proof that you're trying hard.**

  The only way to completely avoid failure is by not trying at all. Failure is proof that you're challenging yourself.

It takes work to turn failure into something positive. But it's possible if you try!

REFLECTION:

What's a time that you failed and bounced back?

_____

_____

_____

How did failure help you do better?

_____

_____

HOW DID MAX GROW STRONGER?

Max didn't want to go to basketball practice. But he also didn't want to let his dad down. That would make him feel like an even bigger failure.

So he packed his bag for the next day. As he filled his water bottle, his dad came over to him and said, "I know you're disappointed. But I also know you can do a great job this season. It doesn't matter what team they put you on. Max, you've got this!"

And he was right! Max did a great job on the B-team that year. He was a top scorer, he made some new friends, and he had fun! He chose to make the best of the situation even though it wasn't what he wanted.

In fact, a little part of him was almost glad he got put on the B-team. He was one of the best players on the team, and he got plenty of playing time! All the work he put in this year might help his chances of making the A-team next year.

Staying on the travel team fueled his love of basketball. So when the season was over, Max decided he wasn't done with basketball after all.

Exercises

THINK BIG

REMEMBER SUCCESSFUL PEOPLE WHO FAILED

There was a day early on in the travel league season when Max's dad told him about Michael Jordan. (Of course Max already knew who Michael Jordan was.) But what Max didn't know is that Michael failed to make his high school varsity basketball team the first time he tried out! Did Michael let that stop him? No! He kept practicing more and more. What was the result? He became one of the greatest basketball players of all time.

Hearing that story inspired Max. He felt better knowing that even the best basketball players get rejected sometimes. Whenever he started feeling bad about not making the A-team, he thought about what Michael Jordan did.

Hearing about a famous failure helped Max feel better. Experts have found that kids actually perform better when they learn that a lot of success stories began with failure.

In one class, teachers told students about great inventors, engineers, and scientists. They kept talking about these people's success and hyping them up! Do you know what happened? The students' grades went down.

So the teachers tried something different. They started telling the students about how these famous people had actually failed many times during their careers.

Have you learned in school about Thomas Edison? He was one of the people who helped invent the lightbulb, and he invented other great things, too. But did you know that he also had over a thousand inventions that didn't work?

When the students learned that people like Thomas Edison had failed many times, their grades went back up. Why? The stories gave them confidence! They now knew that one mistake (or one bad grade) didn't mean they weren't good at science. They could fail and still succeed later.

The next time you're tempted to give up on something because you failed, do a little research. See if you can find an example of a successful person who made similar mistakes.

Here are a few more examples if you need some inspiration:

- **Theodor Geisel (better known as Dr. Seuss)**

  He sent his first book to twenty-seven publishers, and all of them rejected it. A friend finally helped him get a publishing deal, and he went on to write legendary kids' books that have sold over 600 million copies!

- **Oprah Winfrey (one of the most famous talk show hosts in history)**

  Oprah was fired from her first job as a TV news host. Her producer even told her she was unfit for television news. She went on to become the star of the highest rated talk show ever. It was on TV for more than twenty-five years!

- **Walt Disney (creator of Disney World)**

  Before opening Disney World (and even before he created Mickey Mouse), Walt Disney failed many times. He was even fired once because his boss said that "he lacked imagination and had no good ideas." Most of his cartoons were rejected, and some of his first movies flopped. What happened with him? All you need to do is look at all the movies *you loved as a young kid to know how things turned out for Walt Disney!*

You don't have to look very far to find successful singers, athletes, inventors, writers, and actors who failed many times before they made it big. But it's not just famous people that this happens to. Local business owners, community leaders, and maybe even your parents went through failures too before they reached their goals. Ask them about it sometime!

Anytime you fail at something, remind yourself of all these people! Their stories will help you keep going, too.

REFLECTION:

Who is someone who bounced back from failure that can inspire you when you're feeling down?

_____

_____

Feel GOOD

CALL YOURSELF BY NAME

Max's dad didn't give long lectures—he saved his words

for things that were really important. So Max took all the wise words his dad gave him to heart.

One of the things his dad said was, "Max, you've got this!" That sentence echoed in his head all basketball season. Whether he was on the foul line, or he was trying to get a rebound, he would say to himself, "Max, you've got this!"

It seemed to help. And it's no wonder why. There is research that says talking to yourself in the third person can keep you calm.

When you call yourself by your first name, you see an obstacle as a challenge. You don't see it as a threat anymore.

If you don't know how to do a problem on your homework, you might be more likely to figure it out if you call yourself by name.

It's something that professional basketball player LeBron James is known for. Once, he left his hometown team to join a more popular team. Many people accused him of being disloyal, and reporters asked him why he did it. He said, "I wanted to do what's best for LeBron James and to do what makes LeBron James happy."

Viewers thought he was a little strange for talking about himself in the third person. (So you may not want to do this out loud.) But you can refer to yourself by name in your head.

Saying your name to yourself can help you stay calm. And it may help you make the best decisions. This can be key to helping you bounce back after you fail. Try this anytime you're thinking about giving up!

Take a minute to think of a sentence you can repeat to yourself (sort of like the creating your own catch-phrase exercise we talked about in Chapter 2). What can you tell yourself to stay motivated after you've failed at something? Call yourself by name and give yourself a little pep talk in the sentence.

Here are some examples:

- Try again, Alyson. You've got this!
- Keep going, Harper. You can do this!
- Jackson, you've got to make the best decisions you can!

REFLECTION:

What's a saying you can create for yourself that causes you to call yourself by name? Write it down. And say it out loud!

_____

_____

_____

ACT BRAVE

PROVE YOUR BRAIN WRONG

When Max was put on the B-team, he could have easily thought that he wasn't a good basketball player. And he could have just given up. But the only way he would know for sure was to keep trying.

It's important to realize when your brain tries to lie to you. It will try to convince you that you're not good enough, that you can't succeed, or that you shouldn't bother trying. This is especially true after you've failed once.

It's true you can take steps to think bigger and feel better. But sometimes you just have to do something to prove yourself wrong!

This will challenge your brain's negativity. When your brain says you can't do something, respond by thinking, "Challenge accepted!" Then try to do whatever your brain is telling you that you can't do.

Here are a few examples of how you might prove your brain wrong:

- Your brain says you'll never make the soccer team. Try out for the team anyway.
- Your brain says no one will talk to you at a party. Go to the party and start talking to people.

- Your brain says there's no way you're going to pass pre-algebra. Try your best to pass the class.

REFLECTION:

What's an example of a time when your brain tried to convince you that you might fail?

_____

How could you have tried to prove your brain wrong?

_____

Traps to Avoid

You might think you're doing amazing in life if you never fail at anything. But if you never fail, that means there is a pretty good chance that you aren't trying hard things. Remember, failure is proof that you're challenging yourself.

You might also find that you're used to failing in some areas of your life, but not in others. Maybe you fail to place in a swim meet every week, so it doesn't seem like a big deal when you don't get a medal. But if you're used to getting good grades, you might feel crushed if you fail one test. No one succeeds at everything all the time.

Take a look at the times when failing feels the worst.

And then think about what keeps you from trying again. Always remember that failure can be an important step toward success.

11

They Balance Social Time with Alone Time

Madison always had a busy schedule. Between dance, piano lessons, drama club, youth group, and field hockey, she barely had time to do her homework. She always found time for friends though. And since she was in so many activities, she had lots of friends!

Sometimes she felt like she was pulled in too many different directions. It was stressful to run from piano lessons straight to dance class. But her mother helped her out. She drove Madison from one place to the next, and she always showed up with a snack or anything else she might need. They also gave her friends rides to and from activities. She liked that she was always in the middle of everything.

It was almost spring break now. And Madison's family had rented a cabin up north. Her father said they were going to have some quiet family time up there.

Madison didn't really think much about their trip until the night before they left. She was too busy doing other stuff.

But now it was time to pack. She stared at her empty suitcase. She had no idea what to take with her.

She threw a bunch of clothes in there, and she grabbed her tablet. She figured she wouldn't need much else.

The next morning, she and her older brothers climbed into the van. The family headed for the cabin. They had never gone to this place before, so Madison wasn't sure what to expect.

She put her headphones on and fell asleep for most of the ride. An hour later, she woke up and yawned. She reached over to check her phone, but for some reason it wasn't working.

"Does anyone else get a signal?" she asked.

Her older brother laughed and said, "We're in the middle of nowhere, Madison! Your phone hasn't had a signal for a long time."

"Oh!" she said. "Well, wake me up when we get to this cabin. I can wait till then."

Her mother said, "No, honey. We talked about this.

There is no internet or cell service up there. That's one of the reasons why we picked this place—so we can get away from all that for a bit."

"What? We did not talk about this!" Madison said. A feeling of fear washed over her. "I wouldn't have come if I knew I couldn't talk to my friends for a whole week!"

Then her father spoke up and said, "The fact that you're so upset about this tells me you need a break from texting more than ever. It's not good to be glued to your phone all the time. This trip will allow us to spend time together as a family."

Forced family fun? No phone? No internet? No contact with friends? Madison already wished she was back in school.

Check Yourself

It's important to talk to people, spend time with friends, and have a social life. Life would be pretty boring if you didn't! But it's also important to be alone sometimes in order to recharge. Check out these sentences, and see how many of them apply to you:

☐ I think being alone means feeling lonely.

☐ I feel weird doing things by myself.

☐ I would never plan time to be alone on purpose.

- [ ] I have so much going on in my head. I never sit in silence!
- [ ] If there's not someone in the room with me, I'm probably staring at a screen (my phone, TV, or a computer).
- [ ] I sleep with the radio or TV on for background noise.
- [ ] Spending time by myself sounds boring!

The more those statements sound like you, the more difficulty you may have spending time alone. It's important to create a healthy balance in your life between social time and alone time. In this chapter, we'll talk about why alone time is so important.

But first, let's get back to Madison and the family trip. . . .

 ## Closer Look

After what seemed like forever, Madison's family finally arrived at the cabin. She went inside and looked around. The place smelled weird. It was dusty, and the furniture looked old. She checked her phone again—there was still no signal.

"How far will we have to drive to get cell service?" she asked.

Her father sighed and said, "Madison, we're not driving two hours so you can talk to your friends. I can tell you how the conversation will go: 'What's up?'

'Nothing. What's up with you?' 'Nothing.' You're not missing anything if you're out of touch for a few days."

Madison disagreed. Talking to her friends was a vital part of her life! What was she going to do for the next week? Stare at these ugly walls?

Maybe you understand what Madison was going through. There may have been times in your life when you felt like things were going to be too boring or too quiet.

But not all alone time is the same. Sure, being lonely isn't good for you. But having time alone can also be an opportunity to learn more about yourself. When you choose to spend time alone, it doesn't have to be boring or painful. It can help you grow stronger.

You can use your alone time to create goals, imagine changes, or think about your emotions. Here are some examples of what separates time alone from quality time alone:

- **Time alone:** sitting in your room playing video games for hours
- **Quality time alone:** writing in a journal for fifteen minutes

- **Time alone:** binge-watching your favorite Netflix shows
- **Quality time alone:** doing artwork

- **Time alone:** texting your friends while sitting in the back-yard
- **Quality time alone:** taking a nice walk through the woods

Quality time alone might include meditation—but it doesn't have to be about sitting still. It can involve doing anything that gives your mind a chance to relax a little.

It's about having fewer things going into your mind (like the sights and sounds from video games). And it's about allowing your brain a chance to take a break from everything grabbing your attention (like notifications on your phone). You might do a quiet activity you love. Or, you might explore a new place. But the goal is to allow your mind a little break from people.

Of course, some people are more comfortable being alone than others. Some people even prefer to be by themselves. That's okay. But it's important for everyone to learn to make time for both social activities and alone activities.

REFLECTION:

Take a minute to think about the last time you spent quality time by yourself. What did you do?

_____

_____

PROOF POSITIVE

The first twenty-four hours of Madison's spring break were awful! She kept carrying her phone around, even though she didn't have a signal. She kept checking it just in case it started working (it never did).

Since it was too cold to swim, her family sat outside looking at the lake during the day. At night, they played board games and put puzzles together. Madison was bored by it all.

When her father and brothers went fishing, she decided to stay at the cabin with her mother.

She complained, "Mom, this is the worst spring break ever!"

"Well, we are not leaving early. So you might as well make the best of it," her mother said firmly.

Madison knew there was no chance she could enjoy any of this vacation.

But by day three, something started to change. She started feeling a little more comfortable with being separate from the outside world.

She started spending more time with her family. She even read some of the books that were in the cabin. They were not the kind she would normally read back home, but she got completely hooked on a mystery. She went for walks around the cabin, too, and she found some beautiful flowers. She took pictures of them with her phone (at least it was still good for that).

Madison even spent some time in the cabin all by herself while the rest of the family went for a hike. At first it felt really awkward being alone in the cabin. She almost panicked for a minute when she realized she didn't even have a phone to call anyone in an emergency. But then she remembered there was a landline in the kitchen. She could call for help if she really needed it.

She paced around for a bit because she didn't know what to do with herself.

But then she sat down with some paper and a pen. She began to write. She used to write a lot when she was younger, but she hadn't done it in a long time. All it took was a few minutes of writing to remind her how much she loved it.

After that Madison started writing every day at the cabin—pages and pages of stories. It was like she couldn't stop. She would lose track of time, and she even forgot about her phone when she was writing.

By the end of the week, her parents noticed that she seemed calmer and more relaxed than usual. Madison thought about it, and she had to agree. She didn't want to admit it, but maybe she really did need a vacation.

Maybe like Madison, you're used to always being in contact with friends and family members. Even if you don't have a phone, you may be with other people most of the time. Or maybe you constantly entertain yourself with stuff that prevents you from being alone with your thoughts.

Of course, kids aren't the only ones who struggle to find quiet time. Adults often do, too. Sometimes it's because we're too busy. At other times, it just feels too scary or weird to be alone.

Many people assume that being alone is always bad. After all, most of us have been put in time-out by ourselves as punishment at some point in our lives.

But there can be plenty of benefits to being alone:

- **You might be more creative.** Many great artists, musicians, and writers do their best work when they're alone.

- **You can be more productive.** Most people work better when they have a little privacy.

- **You might feel happier.** People who are able to tolerate alone time have more happiness. They are usually less sad or stressed.

- **You might get better grades.** Some experts have found that kids who spend some time alone are more likely to get higher grades.
- **You might get in less trouble.** Many adults think the best way to keep kids out of trouble is to keep them busy. But experts have found that kids who spend time by themselves are less likely to get into trouble. It can feel uncomfortable to be alone when you aren't used to it. Once you get comfortable, though, it can have some serious advantages.

REFLECTION:

When have you spent time alone and enjoyed it?

_____

_____

What did you do during your alone time?

_____

_____

How did it help you?

_____

_____

_____

WHAT MADE MADISON GROW STRONGER?

When Madison returned from spring break, she caught up with her friends and she got back to her routine. But she made one big change. She decided to make time for writing in her schedule!

When she was done with her homework every night, she spent time writing—just for fun. She kept her phone turned off during this time so she could focus.

Madison found that a little quiet time helped her to express herself. She could be as creative as she wanted, and there wasn't any pressure from anyone else.

No one was even reading her stories for now. Maybe she would share them later. But Madison wasn't writing to impress her parents or to get a good grade. She was writing because she loved it!

Exercises

THINK BIG

ZOOM OUT

Writing helped Madison think big! Sure, she wasn't studying. But she was doing something she loved, and she was doing it alone. That gave her energy! It boosted her mood. And it helped give her more energy for other areas of her life.

It's important to find out how you can use a little alone time to help you think big. You might choose to write like Madison did, or you might do something completely different. Whatever you do though, it's important to do it alone. Here's why:

You likely spend a lot of time thinking about certain events going on in your life—an important test, a big game, the school dance.

You might also spend a lot of time thinking about certain people—your family, your friends, someone you have a crush on.

But how much time do you really spend thinking about the big picture stuff—like what you want to be when you grow up or what types of things you want to learn about? Sometimes you have to zoom out and look at the big picture. While you might talk to other people about what you want to do, it's important to spend some time thinking about life on your own. Other people influence you one way or another. Some of them will have a good influence. And some will have a bad influence. But how much influence do you have on yourself?

Can you really get to know yourself if you don't spend time alone? Being alone lets you make decisions without anyone else's input. It's a great time to practice thinking big.

You need some time and space to answer questions like:

- Who am I?
- What do I really like?
- What do I like about myself?
- What do I want to do better?
- Who are the people that are most important to me?
- What do I want to do this week? . . . this month? . . . this year?

When you spend time alone, you can answer these types of questions without being influenced by other people. Just keep in mind that you have a lot of options for how you spend your alone time (we'll talk about that in a minute).

In the meantime, set aside a specific amount of time to be alone with your thoughts. You might schedule ten minutes a day, or you might set aside thirty minutes twice a week. Figure out a schedule that seems like it will work for you. And then make it happen!

REFLECTION:

When can you set aside time to be alone with your thoughts?

_____

_____

What sorts of things would you like to learn about yourself?

_____

_____

_____

_____

Feel GOOD

GET COMFORTABLE BEING UNCOMFORTABLE

Spending quality time alone can be tough if you're not used to it. You might feel bored at first. You might also feel lonely, sad, or anxious.

But this doesn't mean you should quit. Instead, it just means you need practice. Try to keep from picking up your phone, turning on your TV, or talking to your sibling for a few minutes.

When you practice being uncomfortable, you'll learn that you can handle it better than you think. You'll also gain confidence in your ability to do other tough things.

When you are alone, pay attention to your feelings. Notice them and label them (like we talked about in Chapter 3).

Also, notice when you're tempted to give up. Maybe when you start feeling bored you might think, "This is a waste of time." And then you consider calling a friend instead. Or maybe when you feel anxious, you think, "I can't do this." And you're tempted to go talk to someone.

When you feel it happening, remind yourself that you can do this! Although alone time might feel awkward at first, you can do it.

REFLECTION:

How do you feel when you spend time alone?

_____

_____

How can you work through uncomfortable feelings you have?

_____

_____

ACT BRAVE

SCHEDULE SOMETHING FUN TO DO BY YOURSELF

There isn't a set amount of time you should be alone every day or every week. And you don't need to divide your time equally between being alone and being with friends.

Instead, it's important to just create *some* time to do it. You'll need to experiment a bit to figure out how much time is right for you.

You might start with just fifteen minutes each day. Set aside a little time to focus on yourself. You don't have to just sit and stare at the wall. And you don't have to write in a journal or meditate if those things don't sound like something you want to do. (Although you might try them sometime!)

Instead, look for fun things you can do alone. Keep in mind that it's best to avoid your electronics if you can. Most of us already get plenty of screen time, so more time staring at your digital devices isn't going to be helpful.

Here are some examples of ways you can spend quality time by yourself:

- Go for a walk.
- Take pictures in nature.
- Create an art project.
- Work on a puzzle.
- Write down your goals.
- Make a list of things you want to accomplish this year.
- Write in a journal.
- Do yoga.
- Write stories.
- Listen to and make music.

The goal is to pick activities that you enjoy. It's okay if no one else likes to do them. After all, you're doing them for you! Think of it as an opportunity to become friends with yourself.

REFLECTION:

What can you do during your quality time alone?

_____

_____

_____

_____

Traps to Avoid

If you're someone who spends a lot of time alone already, then make sure you're getting enough social time. It's important to be around people, too. Talking to friends and interacting with others is also a big part of being the strongest kid you can be.

So be on the lookout for signs that you're spending too much time alone. Maybe you spend a lot of time in your room, and you get lonely and depressed. This can be a sign that you need to spend more time with people. Or you're kind of shy and it's easier to just spend time alone. It's important to practice talking to people, too.

You might even notice that when you spend a lot of time around people, you get a little grouchy, and you want to be alone. That's okay! A lot of people can feel like that. But make sure you are not spending too much time alone, either. With practice, you will get better at finding the right balance you need in your life to grow stronger.

12

They Are Thankful for What They Have

Abby looked at Riley's clothes and said, "Your outfit is really nice, Riley!" But "nice" felt like an understatement. Her outfit was amazing! But, of course, it had an amazing price tag to go along with it.

Abby knew her mom couldn't afford to buy an outfit like that, but she was used to it by now. Her mom couldn't afford to buy her a lot of the things other parents bought their kids. Her mom also couldn't come to most of her after-school activities. She worked long hours, and she couldn't get out of work early like most parents.

Abby spent a lot of time with her BFF, Riley. Riley's parents were really nice to Abby! They brought her home from games and practices when her mother was working. Sometimes they even brought snacks for her when she and Riley had games. When Abby's mom had to work on Thanksgiving, they invited Abby over to their house to eat with their family.

Abby loved being at Riley's house on Fridays for their family pizza night, too. After they ate, they all usually watched a movie together. Sometimes Abby almost felt like she was part of their family.

One Friday night after they were done watching the movie, Riley's mom said, "Hey, Abby, do you want to check out these clothes? They don't fit Riley anymore. But they might fit you."

Abby said, "Sure!" She picked out a few shirts and a couple pairs of pants that she knew she could wear. "Thank you!" Abby said as she put them in her bag. At the end of the evening, Riley's dad drove Abby home.

When Abby walked in the front door she saw her mother sitting at the kitchen table. She had her head in her hands.

"No matter how hard I work, the pile of bills just gets higher and higher! I just can't get ahead," she said.

Abby put her hand on her mother's shoulder. She said, "It's okay, Mom. You work really hard, and we'll get through this. We always do."

She quietly took the bag of Riley's hand-me-downs to her room. Abby didn't want her mom to see them right now. She thought her mom might feel worse if she knew other people were giving her clothes.

She lay on her bed and stared at the ceiling for a few minutes. She thought about how easy Riley's life was compared to hers. Riley had two parents who could afford to get her nice things. They were a nice family, and they cared about each other.

Abby wished she had a life like that. She was sick of stressing about money and having to calm her mother down. She just wanted to have pizza night and watch movies like Riley's family did!

Check Yourself

Sometimes it's hard to be thankful for what you have. It's easier to think of all the things you don't have. But overlooking the good things in your life can cause bigger problems for you.

Read over the following sentences. See how many of them sound like you.

- ☐ I think more about things I want than the things I already have.
- ☐ I usually talk about what went wrong instead of what went right.

- [ ] I rarely show people I appreciate them.
- [ ] I sometimes feel disappointed with the gifts that people give me.
- [ ] I think I deserve more than I have.
- [ ] I think my life is unfair.
- [ ] I say thank you to be polite, but I don't really feel thankful.

Do many of these sound like you? If so, you are not alone. But it's important to know that being thankful can make you stronger. It can help you become the best version of yourself! In this chapter, we'll discuss why it's important to be thankful for what you have.

But, first, let's get back to Abby. . . .

Closer Look

Abby didn't sleep much that night. Instead, she just kept thinking about how much she wanted a better life. She was sure that she would be happier if they had more money. And she would probably like school more, too, if she had brand-name clothes. She wished she lived in a bigger house with a mom who didn't work so much.

As she tossed and turned, she thought about how she would feel in a family like Riley's. Abby felt happy

Riley had such an awesome life. But she couldn't help feeling a little jealous.

And she would never want her mom to know that she had these kinds of thoughts. She loved her mom, and she knew her mom worked hard! She just didn't have the kind of job that paid a lot of money, and Abby was sad about that.

Maybe you can relate to Abby's experience. Have you ever wondered if your life might be better if you had more stuff (or maybe if you had different parents)?

Thinking this way can cause you to overlook the things you do have.

When we feel thankful for something, it's called gratitude. You might hear people talk about feeling grateful sometimes, especially around holidays like Thanksgiving. But gratitude doesn't need to be saved up for special occasions. It's good to feel anytime!

The difference between being grateful and ungrateful is usually all in the way you choose to look at things.

Here are some examples:

Your parents say you can have five people come to your birthday party.

- **Ungrateful**—"It's not fair! I have ten people I want to invite. I might as well not even have a party if I can only have five people."

- **Grateful**—"I'll think about which friends I want to invite. This is going to be a great party!"

You arrive at the movie theater five minutes after the movie started.

- **Ungrateful**—"I can't believe my parents got us here late. We missed the first few minutes. Now I probably won't understand what's going on in the movie."
- **Grateful**—"I'm happy my parents brought us here tonight. Pass the popcorn. This movie is going to be great!"

It stops raining right before your baseball game starts.

- **Ungrateful**—"Now the field is all muddy. Why did it have to rain today?"
- **Grateful**—"I'm glad it stopped raining before the game started. Now we still get to play today!"

No one is grateful all the time. But you can teach yourself to feel grateful more often. There are a lot of good reasons why you may want to do that. Let's talk about those next.

PROOF POSITIVE

Abby slept in a little bit on Saturday morning. When she woke up, her mother was already at work, so she was home alone as usual.

As she made herself some cereal, she looked out the window. The little kids who lived in the apartment next door were playing on the playground. Their grand-mother was trying to push one of the kids on the swings.

Abby decided she would go join them when she was done eating. She liked to help out the little kids' grand-mother sometimes. She was an older lady who was rais-ing four grandkids by herself. Abby didn't know why the kids lived with their grandmother, but she knew that the grandmother always looked tired. Right now she looked like she could use a little help.

When Abby was done eating, she headed out to the playground.

The grandmother looked at Abby and said, "Thank you so much for coming out here, dear! I'm so lucky that nice kids like you live in this building. The little things you do help me out so much. I have trouble keeping up with all my grandchildren when I'm out here alone. An extra set of hands makes it so much easier!"

Abby kept playing with the kids a little while longer. She helped them cross the monkey bars, she pushed them on the swings, and she caught them at the bottom of the slide. When they were done, even she was tired! She could only imagine how tired their grandmother must feel!

When she went home, she thought more about the sweet grandmother. "She thanked me for helping her," Abby thought.

The grandmother could have complained about how unfair it was that she was raising little kids at her age. Or she could have complained that she usually didn't have help. Instead, she seemed really thankful that Abby took a little bit of time to play with her grandkids.

Abby started to think that she might have things to be grateful for, too.

Maybe you understand Abby's experience. You may have times when you forget about the good stuff going on in your life. It might be because you're so distracted by the bad stuff.

But being grateful for what you have is more than just a nice thing to do. Experts have found that being thankful can be really good for *you* as well.

Here's what they say about gratitude:

- **It can help you make more friends.** People who say thank you usually make a lot more friends. They keep their friends longer, too.
- **It may keep you healthier.** Grateful people usually take better care of their health. They even live longer!
- **It may help you feel happier.** Being a thankful person can make you happier. There is less chance that you will get depressed when you are looking for things to be grateful for.
- **Your self-esteem might improve.** Grateful people feel better about themselves.
- **You might sleep better.** People who practice gratitude sleep better. And they sleep more!

Those are just a few reasons why you might want to bring more gratitude into your life. The good news is that it's easy to be grateful, and you might find that you like it.

REFLECTION:

When is a time when you were thankful for something?

_____

_____

HOW DID ABBY GROW STRONGER?

Slowly Abby began thinking more about her life. And she started looking at things a little bit differently.

She was grateful that:

- She had such a loving and hardworking mother.
- She had a good friend like Riley.
- Riley's parents were so nice to her.
- She got to help the grandmother in her building (and she enjoyed playing with the little kids, too)!

More and more, Abby noticed what she had to be thankful for. She actually had a lot of great things in her life. She didn't even have to look that hard to find them.

This isn't to say that Abby couldn't create a more positive future for herself (like we talked about in Chapter 7). She certainly could! But in the meantime, she could also practice being thankful for what she had.

Being more grateful gave Abby a burst of positivity.

It also gave her more energy to do the things she wanted to do.

Exercises

THINK BIG

LIST THREE THINGS YOU ARE THANKFUL FOR

Just like Abby, you can find things you have to be grateful for in your life. Remember that you don't have to come up with huge things. You can also be thankful for the little things that happen every day, like having lights that turn on or clean water to drink.

The best way to do this is to make a list. It's going to get long! So you might even start keeping a gratitude notebook or journal.

Make it a habit to write down three things you're grateful for every day.

HERE'S A SAMPLE LIST:

Day 1:

- I got to play with my dog.
- I didn't have any homework.
- We ate hamburgers for dinner.

Day 2:

- We had a substitute in math class.
- I went to the park after school.
- I got to watch my favorite show.

Keeping a simple daily list can remind you of all the good things in your life. Later you can look back through your notes again. Then you'll remember how much you have to be grateful for!

When you start making the list, you'll notice that you start looking for the good stuff in your day. All day long you might think, "Add this to the gratitude list!" You'll probably find that it's easier than you think to come up with three good things every day. And writing them down keeps your mind focused on the positive.

REFLECTION:

What are three things you are grateful for today?

1. _____

2. _____

3. _____

When will you start creating your list?

_____

Feel GOOD

ASK, "HOW DO I FEEL ABOUT WHAT I'VE BEEN GIVEN?"

It's easy to say, "Thank you," when someone gives you a gift. But saying thanks doesn't mean you really *feel* grateful.

The best way to feel grateful is to ask yourself how you feel about what someone did for you.

Maybe your grandmother gave you a present for your birthday. Or maybe your friend shared half their sandwich with you. Pause, and ask yourself how you feel. Take a minute to think about those feelings.

Keep in mind that we're not only talking about physical gifts. Maybe a coach made you the captain of the team. Or maybe your parents finally decided you're responsible enough to stay up later. Think about how you feel when you're given these types of gifts, too.

Also, think about how the other person might have felt when they were picking out your gift. Imagine how they felt when they were giving it to you.

Here are some examples:

Your teacher gives you an award for Most Improved Student.

- **You feel:** Proud and happy. You know your teacher picked you out of all the students!
- **Your teacher's feelings:** Your teacher probably feels proud of you, too. She watched your grades get better all year. She did a good job of teaching you!

Your friend shares half his lunch with you.

- **You feel:** Special, happy, and loved. You are glad you have such a good friend. And you know you would do the same for him!
- **Your friend's feelings:** Your friend probably feels happy

that he was able to help you out when you were hungry. He knows you would do the same for him!

Your grandmother gives you a birthday present.

- **You feel:** Loved and important. You picture your grandmother shopping for your gift. She spent her time and money to pick out something she thought would make you happy!
- **Your grandmother's feelings:** Your grandmother probably feels happy that she is able to give a gift to her grandchild. She can't wait to see you use it!

Imagining how the other person felt can remind you how much they care about you. Thinking about them in a positive way can help you feel good about them, too—which is great for your relationship. Sometimes the thought of how much that person cared about you is even better than the gift itself!

REFLECT:

Think about the last time someone gave you a gift. How did you feel?

_____

_____

How do you think that person felt about giving it to you?

_____

_____

ACT BRAVE

SHOW YOUR GRATITUDE

It's one thing to *think* about what you have to be grateful for. It's another thing to *feel* grateful. But *showing* your gratitude is also important!

There are many ways you might show how thankful you are to someone else. A simple way to do this is by paying attention to how you say thank you. Do you just sort of mumble, "Thanks," and walk away? Or do you look the person in the eye and say, "Thank you!" like you mean it?

You can say thank you to the person who serves your food in the cafeteria. You can say it to the kid who hands you a pencil when you forgot yours. Saying thank you these times is important. But it's not the only way to express gratitude.

You can also write someone a thank-you note. Don't

just grab a piece of paper and write, "Thanks for the gift!" Instead, write a note that describes how you felt when you got the gift. Let the person know why you like it so much.

You can also write someone a gratitude letter because you appreciate who they are. You can write a letter to your friend, a parent, a teacher, a coach, or a relative. Don't be afraid to tell them how much they mean to you.

It takes courage to do that! You might worry that someone will think you are weird. Or you might worry that they don't feel the same about you. But sharing your gratitude with them will help them feel good. It might even change their life!

You can also write gratitude letters to people you don't even know personally. For example, you might send a thank-you note to the ambulance workers and firefighters who took care of everyone after a disaster. Or you might leave a little note for the person who picks up your garbage every week (even if you don't ever see them). Tell people that they are doing a good job! Tell them you appreciate their work! It can help them feel good, and it will make you feel good to spread the gratitude around.

REFLECTION:

Who is someone in your life that you want to show gratitude?

_____

_____

How can you express your gratitude to them?

_____

_____

Traps to Avoid

Your parents might have gratitude rituals (some families do). They might ask you what you're thankful for at dinner. Or they might want you to share the best part of your day.

Talking about gratitude and making it a daily habit is a good idea. But you might think it feels a little bit forced when someone always asks you what you're grateful for. You might find it's helpful to do something on your own, too. A private gratitude journal might be what really helps you feel thankful.

Saying thank you can become a habit also. When it becomes a habit, it doesn't really mean much. So be aware that you might say thank you a lot without really feeling gratitude. Work on finding ways to express real gratitude! A smile or a fist bump (along with the words "thank you") might be more real.

QUICK TIPS

Strong kids are thankful for what they have—both big and little things. But it's tough to have gratitude sometimes. The next time you're struggling to be thankful, remember these exercises can help you think big, feel good, and act brave.

THINK BIG: Make a list of three things you feel grateful for. Look at it every now and then to remind yourself of all you have to be thankful for!

Feel GOOD: When someone gives you a gift, don't just say thank you. Really think about how you feel. It will help you experience real gratitude!

ACT BRAVE: Express your gratitude to others. Tell other people how you feel! Write letters of appreciation!

13

They Persist

Michael was waiting in line to get on the bus. He saw his friends coming, so he tried to turn his back quickly, hoping they wouldn't see him when they walked by.

Every Friday, they all walked to the pizza place together. It sounded like they had a lot of fun. Sometimes they would even chill at someone's house afterward.

But Michael only knew all this because he heard stories about it. He wasn't allowed to go.

When he asked to join them, his parents would say, "No. You're not going to run around town on your own," or "We can't let you be unsupervised." Every week Michael cringed as his friends walked past him on their way to have fun while he waited for the bus.

The bus line started moving, and Michael breathed a sigh of relief. But just as he thought that he was home free, one of his friends yelled, "See you Monday, Mike!"

He turned around and saw the guys walking together. So he waved and forced a smile.

They never made fun of him for not being able to go—but Michael still felt embarrassed that his parents wouldn't let him join.

He stared out the window the whole ride home. When the bus reached his stop, he grabbed his backpack and trudged home.

When Michael walked in the door, he immediately said, "Mom, I'd much rather be hanging out with my friends and eating pizza right now! When are you going to let me hang out with them after school?"

His mother said, "Honey, we've talked about this. Your father and I feel like you're still a little too young to walk around town by yourself."

Michael sighed. "But, Mom . . . everyone else's parents trust them! Why can't you and Dad trust me, too?"

She answered, "Let's talk about it when your father gets home." Michael sighed again and went to his room. He didn't think they were ever going to trust him!

But over dinner that night, he brought up the subject again. "Dad, Mom said we can talk about when you two are going to trust me enough to go hang out with my friends after school."

His dad said, "Michael, it's not that we don't trust you. We don't think you would purposely do something wrong. We just wonder about your decision-making sometimes, and we aren't sure if you are responsible enough to be out on your own."

"Wait! What do you mean I'm not responsible enough, Dad?" Michael asked.

"Well, you forget to do basic things sometimes— like clean your room. And if your mother didn't remind you to do your homework, you probably wouldn't do that either," his father said.

"What does cleaning my room have to do with walking around with my friends? I don't get it," Michael said.

His father said, "Well, if you're not mature enough to make your bed, how do we know you'll be mature enough to say no if your friends dare you to do something dangerous? If you struggle to make good choices when you're at home, then how do we know you'll make good choices when there isn't an adult around? When you show us you can be responsible, that's when we'll give you more responsibility."

"Fine! I'll show you I can be responsible," Michael said.

The next morning, Michael made his bed before he came out of his room. Right after breakfast he went back to his room and started cleaning. Although he wasn't going to admit it out loud, he had to agree his room was a mess.

So Michael spent a few hours getting things organized. He picked up piles of dirty clothes, sorted through old papers, and got rid of stuff he didn't need. When he was done, he stepped back and smiled!

"Mom! Dad! Come look!" he yelled. When they showed up at his door, he said, "Check it out! It's all clean. Told you I'm responsible!"

"That looks great, Michael. Now keep it up," his dad said.

"I will! But this means I can go out with my friends next Friday, right?" Michael asked.

His father said, "No, Michael. Cleaning your room one time doesn't mean you're responsible. You have to show us you can be responsible over time."

"Well, why would I keep cleaning my room every day if it isn't going to get me anything?" Michael said.

To that, his father replied, "If you can't persist at something for more than one day, I'll take it as proof you're not mature enough to be unsupervised with your friends, Michael."

Michael flopped down on his bed. How on earth was he going to show his parents he was responsible—and persistent—before next Friday?

Check Yourself

It's hard to be persistent sometimes. We want everything to happen right away. But being impatient can cause a lot of bigger problems in our lives. Check out the following statements and see how many of them sound like you.

- ☐ I give up if things get too hard.
- ☐ If it's going to take a long time to reach a goal, I don't bother to start.
- ☐ When I'm trying to get better at something, I need to see improvements right away.
- ☐ When I want something, I want it now.
- ☐ I have trouble sticking to my goals.
- ☐ I look for shortcuts to get things done fast.
- ☐ I underestimate how long things are going to take.

How many of these things sound like you? The more they sound like you, the more trouble you might have persisting when you face tough challenges. In this chapter, we'll talk about what persistence really means, how it helps, and the exercises that can help you become a more persistent person.

But first, let's get back to Michael and his parents. . . .

Closer Look

Michael had been asking his parents if he could hang out with his friends after school for several weeks now. And while they reminded him the whole time that he needed to be more responsible, he wasn't doing anything different.

But as soon as he took action to clean his room, he expected his parents to see him as responsible. What he didn't realize was that he needed to work at it longer if he was going to prove to them that he had changed his ways!

Have you ever felt like Michael? Perhaps you've tried to create a change in your life, too, and you wanted it to happen fast. Maybe it meant showing other people that you've changed (like in Michael's story). Perhaps you had to rebuild trust after you broke it, or you had to show people that you're really going to do what you say.

Many kids feel this way when they want to do something different—like learn a new sport. Other kids might want to create a new goal—like saving up enough money to buy something special. But all these examples have one thing in common. They require persistence!

The dictionary defines persistence as "continuing over a long period," or "continuing when you have difficulty." It's about being willing to keep going (even when things are hard) and continuing to work toward a goal (even when you're tempted to give up).

But not everyone understands what it means to be persistent.

Here are some examples of how people get confused about persistence:

SITUATION: You're learning how to play the guitar.

- **Persistence**—You practice for thirty minutes every day. After a few weeks, you notice you are getting better!
- **Impatience**—You watch videos on YouTube of some really good guitar players. You think you'll never play that well! You might decide to quit right now.

SITUATION: You ask your teacher about some extra help. She said she'll get back to you on when she can meet. But it's been two weeks, and she hasn't mentioned it again.

- **Persistence**—You ask her again if there's a good time to meet (she may have forgotten).
- **Doing nothing**—You decide to just wait until she says something to you again.

SITUATION: You're saving money to buy a new video game.

- **Persistence**—You set aside a little bit of your allowance every week to put in your video game stash.
- **Making an excuse**—You barely save any money. You tell yourself you're being patient. (But really you just aren't doing any work toward your goal.)

As you can see, being persistent isn't the same as giving up, doing nothing, making excuses, or continuing to do something even when it isn't good for you. It's about choosing to keep going even when things take longer than you would like.

 REFLECTION:

What's a time when you weren't persistent?

_____

_____

 PROOF POSITIVE

Michael wanted to hang out with friends ASAP! But his impatience was just more proof to his parents that he wasn't ready to handle more responsibility.

It's tough to be persistent sometimes—for both big

things and small things. Maybe you get so frustrated that you give up whenever things don't go your way. Or maybe you just grow impatient when you don't see big changes fast enough.

Experts have spent a lot of time studying how important it is for kids to learn patience and persistence. And they found that it can make a really big difference in their lives!

In one study, researchers asked thirteen-year-olds whether they wanted $140 now or $1,400 in five years. Then they followed up with those kids to see what happened to them.

The teens who said they were willing to wait and get more money later got better grades in real life. They were also less likely to get in trouble at school (or even with the police). The patient kids also earned more money when they were adults, and they were more likely to be healthy.

So to sum it all up, the experts learned that patient and persistent kids grow up to be happier, healthier, and wealthier adults! How is that for motivation to work on learning to have more patience and persistence now?

Of course, you don't have to wait until you're an adult to see what happens if you lack persistence.

Here are some problems you might experience right now if you struggle to do hard things and stick to your goals:

- **You might be tempted to take bad shortcuts.** Sometimes you can take a shortcut that is sort of fun (like using a cheat code in a video game). But other times impatience can lead to bad shortcuts—like copying your friend's answers instead of doing your own work.

- **You view obstacles as roadblocks.** Whether you were out sick the day the teacher explained how to do a project, or you got a flat tire on your bike, those things can be real problems. Without persistence you might not even try to find solutions to those problems.

- **You might quit early.** It's important to have realistic expectations for yourself. If you expect to become the best musician or the star player overnight, you are forgetting something very important. It takes time and hard work to get better—and you need patience to get through it! If you lack persistence, you might quit too soon because you think you'll never be good enough.

- **You struggle to reach big goals.** Little goals (like getting your homework done) might not take much time. But big goals (like saving money) can take a lot longer. And if you're not persistent, you'll likely get frustrated and lose the motivation you need to keep going every day.

Fortunately, persistence is something we can all learn and practice. And when you become more persistent you might find that you can reach some really cool goals.

REFLECTION:

What's an example of a time when you gave up too soon?

_____

_____

What problems did you have because you weren't persistent?

_____

_____

HOW DID MICHAEL GROW STRONGER?

Michael lay on his bed wondering what he could do to show his parents he was a responsible kid. He felt stuck though. It wasn't like he could make his bed a bunch of times every day. And he couldn't clean his room again—it was already spotless!

He thought about it for a while and decided he needed something a little extra to really show his parents he was responsible. He walked out to the kitchen and found his father. "Hey, Dad! Can I wash your car?"

"Sure, if you want to!" his dad said.

Michael found a bucket and the special soap his dad used to wash the car. He turned on the hose and got to work! He scrubbed and scrubbed. And then he rinsed it off really well. He even dried it so that there wouldn't be any water spots.

When he was done, he went to find his dad. "Hey, Dad, come see how your car looks!"

His dad came outside and said, "Whoa, that looks great, Michael. Thank you so much for doing that!"

Michael smiled and said, "You're welcome. So . . . do you think I can hang out with my friends next Friday now? After all, if I'm responsible enough to wash your car, then I'm responsible enough to hang out with my friends, right?"

His dad shook his head and said, "No, Michael. It doesn't work like that. Just because you can clean your room and wash the car in one day doesn't show us that you're truly responsible. You need to show us you can be responsible every day for a while."

Michael looked up at the sky. He took a deep breath and said, "Dad, I have no idea what you mean by 'a while.' Is that like three days? . . . three months? . . . three years?"

His father said, "I tell you what. If you can show that you can be responsible for two weeks by doing all your chores and getting all your homework done—without a single reminder—then we'll let you go out with your friends."

Michael thought two weeks was an awfully long time. But it also gave him something to try for. If he could just stay focused on doing his chores and his homework, then he could finally hang out with his friends!

He knew he couldn't mess this up! His parents were giving him one shot to show he could do it. And he had to be patient if he wanted them to believe he had really changed his ways.

So he came up with a plan to help him stay motivated. He made the wallpaper on his phone a piece of pizza. Whenever he was tempted to skip his chores or put off his homework, he looked down at his phone and remembered how much he wanted to go have pizza with his friends after school.

And it worked! Every day Michael did chores and got his homework done. And every day when his work was complete, he knew he was one day closer to enjoying more freedom! Of course, the two weeks seemed to go by slower than ever at times. But he stuck with it.

And it was worth it! When the two weeks were up, his mom said, "Michael, you did it! You showed us that you can be a mature young man when you set your mind to it. This Friday, you can go to the pizza spot with your friends after school."

A slow smile spread across Michael's face. He felt a huge sense of relief, and he was so proud of himself. He had done it! What felt nearly impossible two weeks ago was now a reality. He'd stuck it out and convinced his parents he was a responsible, persistent kid who could handle a big privilege!

Exercises

THINK BIG

MAKE A LIST OF REASONS WHY

Michael used the picture of the pizza to remind him of the reasons he should keep doing his chores and homework, even when he didn't feel like it. Seeing that reward on his phone reminded him that if he did the hard work now, he could enjoy the benefits later.

Like Michael, you might feel excited and determined to finish a goal. But you might not feel so excited about the hard work it will take to get there.

After all, it's fun to win a trophy! But practicing is hard—and it can be boring. And showing off a new skill is pretty cool! But *learning* that new skill can be frustrating.

Those uncomfortable emotions may cause you to grow impatient. You might stop putting in much effort. You might look for a shortcut. Or you might even give up!

You might find yourself thinking things like, "What's the use?" or "This is going to take forever!"

The best way to fight off these negative thoughts is by making a list of reasons why you should keep trying. Reading over that list should help keep you going. It can give you the boost you need to get back on track.

Here's an example of someone's list of reasons why they should keep practicing the piano even when it's really hard:

1. I'm getting better slowly!
2. I feel better after I practice!
3. I like knowing how to play the piano—and I'll probably like it even more once I get better!
4. Recitals are fun!
5. It's exciting to learn new songs!

Reading over this list can help this kid fight any thoughts they might have about quitting! What are you going to put on your list?

REFLECTION:

What's a goal you want to reach?

_____

_____

What are five reasons you should keep going when you're tempted to give up?

1. _____

2. _____

3. _____

4. _____

5. _____

FEEL GOOD: WRITE YOURSELF A KIND LETTER

Michael may have benefited from writing himself a kind letter. On the days when he was hard on himself (or the times when he felt like giving up), reading a letter to himself could have given him a boost of motivation.

When you're working on a goal and things get tough, you might be hard on yourself. Maybe you even call yourself names, or you tell yourself that you can't do something. These types of negative thoughts can make you feel bad.

One of the kindest things you can do for yourself is to write yourself a nice letter. Your letter might sound like the kind things your parents or friends would tell *you* when you're upset. (This is similar to talking to yourself like a good friend, as we talked about in Chapter 7.) It's up to you to decide how long or how short you make your letter. It's *to* you and *from* you!

Here's an example of someone's kind letter to herself:

> Dear Lauren,
>
> I know you are having a tough time. And I know you're tempted to give up because you're tired and the work is really tough. And sometimes you don't believe you're good enough.
>
> But the truth is that you are awesome! You are smart. You are kind. And you are loved, even though you don't always feel that way.
>
> No matter what happens, be brave! You can do hard things. You've done them before. I believe in you because you are a unique kid who is going to make this world a better place someday.
>
> Not everyone will recognize how great you are. And that's okay. As long as you know you can do it, you will make good things happen! Just keep going, even when you don't feel like it. You can do it!
>
> Sincerely,
>
> Lauren

When you're done with your letter, keep it in a safe place. Put it in your nightstand, tuck it away in a book, or put it in your backpack. And when you're having one of those days when you're tempted to give up, take out your letter. Reading it can help you feel better and give you an extra boost of motivation so you can keep going.

REFLECTION:

What are some things you want to include in your kind letter to yourself?

_____

_____

_____

ACT BRAVE

CREATE A GOAL YOU CAN MEASURE (AND TRACK YOUR PROGRESS)

Michael struggled the most when he didn't have a timeline. His father told him he had to show he was responsible for "a while," but didn't explain his definition of "a while." Michael did much better once his dad put a timeline on it.

That's because it's easier to have more patience when we know how long something will take. After all, you wouldn't want to run a race if you had no idea how long you had to run or where the finish line was, would you?

The same can be said about any of your goals. It's

easier to be persistent when you have a real goal you can measure—and when you have a way to track your progress.

We will call goals that we can't reach "fuzzy goals." Here's how you might turn a fuzzy goal into a measurable goal.

- **Fuzzy goal:** I want to eat healthier.
- **Measurable goal:** I want to eat three vegetables every day.

- **Fuzzy goal:** I want to get in better shape.
- **Measurable goal:** I want to run one mile every day.

- **Fuzzy goal:** I want to get better at soccer.
- **Measurable goal:** I want to practice soccer for thirty minutes a day, five days a week.

Experts have found that people reach their goals much easier when they keep track of their progress. So find a simple way to track the work you're putting in to reach your goals.

Here are some ways you might do that:

- Put a checkmark on the calendar every day you spend thirty minutes practicing your trumpet.
- Make a poster for your wall with a graph that helps you

track how much money you're making.

- Time yourself every day when you run the mile.

Traps to Avoid

There may be times when you think, "Yeah, but impatience works better than persistence!" When you tell your little brother to hurry up, he might hurry! Acting impatient may work in the short-term sometimes—it might get other people to move a little faster. But there are consequences to that. Other people might also not like you very much. After all, when is the last time you said, "You know what I really like about that person? He's so impatient!"

There may be times when you feel like you just can't handle the frustration when you try to persist.

You might think, "I can't stand to do this any longer!" or "Practicing for ten more minutes feels impossible!" When you feel yourself getting irritated, use an exercise that will help you calm down (like "smell the pizza" or using your calm-down kit).

There may also be times when you decide it doesn't make sense to keep being persistent in certain situations. If your friend is thirty minutes late, you might decide to leave.

Or you might decide that the benefit just doesn't outweigh the amount of work you'd have to put in to reaching a certain goal. These times are okay, too. Just make sure you're not quitting because you doubt your ability or you don't want to handle feeling frustrated!

Don't confuse persistence with unhealthy stubbornness. If you keep losing at an arcade game, don't keep wasting money on it because you're determined to win eventually. If a goal isn't good for you, or it's causing too many problems in your life, you might decide to change course, rather than keep persisting.

QUICK TIPS

Strong kids are persistent! They don't look at tough times as obstacles. They look at them as challenges they can overcome. Of course, it's hard to keep going when you don't feel like it. But the next time you're tempted to give up, remember these exercises that can help you think big, feel good, and act brave.

THINK BIG : When you set a new goal for yourself, create a list of reasons why you should keep going. On the days when you're tempted to give up, read over the list.

Feel GOOD : Write yourself a kind letter. Read it over whenever you need to remind yourself that you can do hard things.

ACT BRAVE : Create a measurable goal for yourself and find a way to track your progress.

Conclusion

Congratulations! You have finished reading this book. We've covered a lot of ground. And by now you've learned forty-two different exercises that will help you build the mental muscles you need to be your best!

Of course, reading this book didn't make you strong. Just like reading a book about how to build big arm muscles won't give you biceps (unless it's a really heavy book), reading this book won't automatically make you mentally strong.

You have to keep exercising if you want to grow strong—and stay strong! Now that you know the exercises that build mental muscles, you can keep doing them on your own.

You'll likely have some favorite exercises that you

come back to regularly. And there may be some others you forget over time. But don't worry. You can always get this book out whenever you need a little reminder.

Sometimes it's easier when you can see all the exercises in one place. Here are all the exercises we practiced:

THINK BIG

- Play to Win!
- Turn BLUE Thoughts into True Thoughts
- Create Your Catchphrase
- Look for the Silver Lining
- "Change the Channel"
- Give it the "Give Up" Test
- Argue the Opposite
- Talk to Yourself Like a Good Friend
- Replace Problem Thoughts with Solution Thoughts
- Open the Shoebox
- Remember Successful People Who Failed
- Zoom Out
- List Three Things You Are Thankful For
- Make a List of Reasons Why

FEEL GOOD

- Think of Five Trusted People You Can Talk To
- Are Your Feelings a Friend or an Enemy?

- Think Before You Feel
- Name Your Feelings
- Schedule Time to Worry
- Smell the Pizza
- Test Your Anxiety Alarm
- Create an "If . . . Then" Plan
- Create a Calm-Down Kit
- "Walk a Mile in Someone Else's Shoes"
- Call Yourself by Name
- Get Comfortable Being Uncomfortable
- Ask, "How Do I Feel About What I've Been Given?"
- Write Yourself a Kind Letter

ACT BRAVE

- Perform Experiments
- Pick a Mood Booster
- Use Empowering Words
- Practice STEPS to Problem-Solving
- Charge Your Batteries
- Deliver a Polite No
- Listen to Your "Shoulder Angel"
- Find Your People
- Set Yourself Up for Success
- Act Like the Type of Person You Want to Be
- Prove Your Brain Wrong

- Schedule Something Fun to Do by Yourself
- Show Your Gratitude
- Create a Goal You Can Measure (and Track Your Progress)

You can mix and match the exercises from different chapters to attack whatever challenges you face. Keep in mind that there's always more than one way to fix a problem.

Here are a few examples of how you could use different exercises to solve the same problem (and help yourself feel better). You might use one exercise or a combination of exercises to help you think big, feel good, or act brave:

PROBLEM: Your friend can only invite five people to their birthday party. You don't get invited, and you feel bad.
You could:
- Pick a mood booster.
- Change the channel in your brain.
- Write yourself a kind letter.

PROBLEM: You get in trouble for something you didn't do, and you're upset.
You could:

- Use your calm-down kit.
- Smell the pizza.
- Use the STEPS to problem-solving.

PROBLEM: Your friends are better than you at a sport. You could:

- Ask yourself if your feelings are a friend or an enemy.
- Talk to yourself like a good friend.
- Replace BLUE thoughts with true thoughts.

Pick an exercise and give it a try. If it doesn't fix the problem (or how you feel about the problem), then try another exercise. Keep in mind that every exercise you do will help you build bigger mental muscles!

COACH YOURSELF

You probably have a coach to teach you how to get better at soccer or how to improve your basketball game. But you probably won't have a coach to help you "up" your mental strength game. Fortunately, you can be your own mental strength coach!

Check in with yourself every day about how you're doing. Are you thinking big? Feeling good? And acting brave? If not, you'll know you have a little work to do to build more strength.

Remember, you don't need to wait until you're struggling to start the exercises! (You wouldn't wait until you need to lift something heavy to start working out your muscles, would you?) Practice a few mental strength exercises every single day, so you can maintain strong mental muscles and make them even bigger!

BECOMING THE STRONGEST YOU

Becoming the strongest you will take hard work! It won't always be fun. But it will be worth the effort.

Remember that many adults wish they had learned these things when they were young. But you know these things now. So you're way ahead of the game already!

If you keep practicing these exercises, you'll build the mental strength you need to live a great life! You'll be brave enough to try new things. You'll also feel good about who you are and what you're capable of doing. And you'll know how to talk to yourself in a helpful way.

When you do the things strong kids do, you can accomplish incredible feats! Whether your goal is to become a kind person who changes *someone else's world*, or you aim to become a scientist who changes the *whole world*, you'll need mental strength to make either of those happen.

Developing bigger mental muscles will give you the courage you need to handle uncomfortable feelings. Imagine what you can accomplish when you dare to face your fears! And picture all the things you'll be able to do because you know how to deal with negative thoughts. You'll be braver than ever before.

This doesn't mean you won't ever question if you're good enough. And it won't mean that you won't be tempted to give up when you fail (everyone does). But now you will have the skills you need to overcome those challenges!

Of course, there will always be obstacles that try to stop you from reaching your goals. But the bigger your mental muscles, the more powerful you'll be. And you'll be able to remind yourself, "I'm strong enough to handle life's toughest challenges!"

If you are reading this book, it's proof that you are already a pretty strong kid who wants to become even stronger. And now you know the exercises you can do to make yourself better. So get out there, and keep working on them! We want you to show the world the very strongest version of you!

References

Introduction

Lane, Andrew M., Peter Totterdell, Ian Macdonald, Tracey J. Devonport, Andrew P. Friesen, Christopher J. Beedie, Damian Stanley, and Alan Nevill. "Brief Online Training Enhances Competitive Performance: Findings of the BBC Lab UK Psychological Skills Intervention Study." *Frontiers in Psychology* 7 (March 30, 2016). https://doi.org/10.3389/fpsyg.2016.00413

Chapter 1

Chorpita, Bruce F., and John R. Weisz. *MATCH-ADTC: Modular Approach to Therapy for Children with Anxiety, Depression, Trauma, or Conduct Problems*. Satellite Beach, FL: PracticeWise (2009).

Chapter 2

Berkovich-Ohana, Aviva, Meytal Wilf, Roni Kahana, Amos Arieli, and Rafael Malach. "Repetitive Speech Elicits Widespread Deactivation in the Human Cortex: the 'Mantra' Effect?" *Brain and Behavior* 5 (7) (May 4, 2015). https://doi.org/10.1002/brb3.346

Chapter 3

Chorpita, Bruce F., and John R. Weisz. *MATCH-ADTC: Modular Approach to Therapy for Children with Anxiety, Depression, Trauma, or Conduct Problems*. Satellite Beach, FL: PracticeWise (2009).

University of California, Los Angeles. "Putting Feelings into Words Produces Therapeutic Effects in the Brain." ScienceDaily. www.sciencedaily.com/releases/2007/06/070622090727.htm

Chapter 4

McGowan, Sarah Kate, and Evelyn Behar. "A Preliminary Investigation of Stimulus Control Training for Worry." *Behavior Modification* 37 (1) (December 2012): 90–112. https://doi.org/10.1177/0145445512455661

Chorpita, Bruce F., and John R. Weisz. *MATCH-ADTC: Modular Approach to Therapy for Children with Anxiety, Depression, Trauma, or Conduct Problems*. Satellite Beach, FL: PracticeWise (2009).

Chapter 5

Nikel, Łukasz. "Submissiveness, Assertiveness and Aggressiveness in School-Age Children: The Role of Self-Efficacy and the Big Five." *Children and Youth Services Review* 110 (March 2020): 104746. https://doi.org/10.1016/j.childyouth.2020.104746

Chorpita, Bruce F., and John R. Weisz. *MATCH-ADTC: Modular Approach to Therapy for Children with Anxiety, Depression, Trauma, or Conduct Problems*. Satellite Beach, FL: PracticeWise (2009).

Chapter 6

Moyses, Kendra. "Helping Children Calm Down." MSU Extension (November 19, 2018). https://www.canr.msu.edu/news/helping_children_calm_down

Chapter 7

Stoeber, Joachim, Aneta V. Lalova, and Ellen J. Lumley. "Perfectionism, (Self-)Compassion,

and Subjective Well-Being: A Mediation Model."
Personality and Individual Differences 154 (2020):
109708. https://doi.org/10.1016/j.paid.2019.109708

Chapter 8

Society for Personality and Social Psychology.
"How we form habits, change existing ones."
ScienceDaily. www.sciencedaily.com/releases
/2014/08/140808111931.htm

Chapter 9

Pfeifer, Jennifer H., Marco Iacoboni, John C.
Mazziotta, and Mirella Dapretto. "Mirroring Others'
Emotions Relates to Empathy and Interpersonal
Competence in Children." *NeuroImage* 39 (4)
(February 15, 2008): 2076–85. https://doi
.org/10.1016/j.neuroimage.2007.10.032

Chapter 10

Lin-Siegler, Xiaodong, Janet N. Ahn, Jondou
Chen, Fu-Fen Anny Fang, and Myra Luna-Lucero.
"Even Einstein Struggled: Effects of Learning about
Great Scientists' Struggles on High School Students'
Motivation to Learn Science." *Journal of Educational
Psychology* 108 (3) (2016): 314–28. https://doi

.org/10.1037/edu0000092

Pease, Donald E. *Theodor Geisel—a Portrait of the Man Who Became Dr. Seuss*. Oxford University Press Inc (2016).

Tate, Amethyst. "Celebs Who Went from Failures to Success Stories." CBS News. CBS Interactive (July 25, 2012). https://www.cbsnews.com/pictures/celebs-who-went-from-failures-to-success-stories/10/

Tate, Amethyst. "Celebs Who Went from Failures to Success Stories." CBS News. CBS Interactive (July 25, 2012). https://www.cbsnews.com/pictures/celebs-who-went-from-failures-to-success-stories/15/

Bruehlman-Senecal, Emma, Ozlem Ayduk, and Ethan Kross. "Self-Talk as a Regulatory Mechanism: How You Do It Matters." *Journal of Personality and Social Psychology* 106 (2) (2014): 304–24. https://doi.org/10.1037/e578192014-452

Chapter 11

Larson, R. W. "The emergence of solitude as a constructive domain of experience in early adolescence." *Child Development* 68 (1) (1997): 80–93. https://doi.org/10.2307/1131927

Long, Christopher R., and James R. Averill. "Solitude: An Exploration of Benefits of Being Alone." *Journal for the Theory of Social Behaviour* 33 (1) (March 5, 2003): 21–44. https://doi.org/10.1111/1468-5914.00204

Manalastas, E. J. "An exercise to teach the psychological benefits of solitude: The date with the self." *Philippine Journal of Psychology* 44 (1) (2011): 95–106.

Chapter 12

Froh, J. J., W. J. Sefick, and R. A. Emmons. "Counting blessings in early adolescents: An experimental study of gratitude and subjective well-being." *Journal of School Psychology* 46(2) (2008): 212–33. https://doi:10.1016/j.jsp.2007.03.005

Nguyen, S. P. and C. L. Gordon. "The Relationship Between Gratitude and Happiness in Young Children." *Journal of Happiness Studies.* (November 2019).

https://doi:10.1007/s10902-019-00188-6

Froh, J. J., J. Fan, R. A. Emmons, G. Bono,
E. S. Huebner, P. Watkins. "Measuring Gratitude
in Youth: Assessing the Psychometric Properties of
Adult Gratitude Scales in Children and Adolescents."
Psychological Assessment 23(2) (2011): 311–24.
https://doi:10.1037/e711892011-001

Chapter 13

Golsteyn, B. H., H. Grönqvist, and L. Lindahl.
"Adolescent Time Preferences Predict Lifetime
Outcomes." *Econ. J.* 124 (2014): F739-F761.
https://doi:10.1111/ecoj.12095

Harkin, Benjamin, Thomas L. Webb, Betty P. I.
Chang, Andrew Prestwich, Mark Conner, Ian Kellar,
Yael Benn, and Paschal Sheeran. "Does Monitoring
Goal Progress Promote Goal Attainment? A Meta-
Analysis of the Experimental Evidence." *Psychological
Bulletin* (2015). https://doi: 10.1037/bul0000025

Zessin, Ulli, Oliver Dickhäuser, and Sven Garbade.
"The Relationship Between Self-Compassion and

Well-Being: A Meta-Analysis." *Applied Psychology: Health and Well-Being* 7 (3) (November 2015): 340–64. https://doi.org/10.1111/aphw.12051

Acknowledgments

Writing a mental strength book for kids has been a dream come true. And I am grateful to the many people who made it possible.

First, I'd like to thank Lisa Sharkey at HarperCollins. She has supported my message and my career as an author since the very beginning. And it was she who introduced my work to the children's division at HarperCollins.

I'd like to thank my editor, Alyson Day, for bringing this project to life. Her support helped me create a better book. And I'm grateful to everyone on the Harper-Collins team who has worked with me over the years to reach new audiences with my books on mental strength.

My agent, Stacey Glick, also gets a huge thank-you. As with my previous books, she's been instrumental in helping me every step along the way. I'm forever grateful that she has helped me spread my message on mental strength in ways I never imagined possible.

I'm also grateful to Nick Valentin for all his help behind the scenes. Not only is he my audio engineer for the *Mentally Strong People* podcast, but he also read through every draft of this manuscript and helped me improve it, word by word (and comma by comma). #outloudtest

Thank you to Steve Cohen and Julie Hintgen, who volunteered to give me feedback on my earliest draft.

I'd also like to thank my junior editorial team. Lauren and Megan House and Abby and Anna Randall gave valuable advice about how to make each chapter kid friendly. And I appreciate all the kids who shared their opinions about the cover, the title, and the illustrations—Ian and Liam Saunders; Meg and Jack Morrison; Leo Hintgen; Silvia Shim; Rex, Quincy, and Vinny Morin; and Sean and Liam Cannon.

Of course, a big thank-you goes to Steve. Whether he's helping me brainstorm a new idea, or he's delivering coffee when I'm writing late at night, he tirelessly supports my career.

Finally, I'm grateful to all my friends and family who encourage my writing and cheer me on.

Photo by Sonya Revell

Amy Morin

is a licensed clinical social worker, instructor at Northeastern University, and psychotherapist. She is the author of the international bestseller *13 Things Mentally Strong People Don't Do*, *13 Things Mentally Strong Parents Don't Do*, and *13 Things Mentally Strong Women Don't Do*. Amy is the editor in chief of Verywell Mind and she's the host of the popular podcast *Mentally Strong People*. She gave one of the most viewed TEDx talks of all time and was named the "self-help guru of the moment" by the *Guardian*. She lives in Marathon, Florida. *13 Things Strong Kids Do* is her fourth book.

You can visit her online at www.amymorinlcsw.com.